FINDING OUR PLACE IN NATURE: ARISTOTLE FOR ENVIRONMENTAL SCIENTISTS

FINDING OUR PLACE

NATURE

ARISTOTLE FOR ENVIRONMENTAL SCIENTISTS

RICHARD LYNN SHEARMAN

RIT
RIT Press

RIT PRESS
ROCHESTER, NEW YORK

Chapter 5 is a revised version of a paper originally published under the title "Can We Be Friends of the Earth?", in the journal *Environmental Values Vol. 14, No. 4* (November 2005), pp. 503-512.

RIT Press
90 Lomb Memorial Drive
Rochester, NY 14623-5604
http://ritpress.rit.edu

ISBN 978-1-939125-62-0 (print)
ISBN 978-1-939125-63-7 (ebook)

Printed in the U.S.A.

Library of Congress Cataloging-in-Publication Data

Names: Shearman, Richard Lynn, 1956- author.
Title: Finding our place in nature : Aristotle for environmental scientists / Richard Lynn Shearman.
Description: Rochester : RIT Press, 2019. | Includes bibliographical references and index. | Summary: "Finding Our Place in Nature argues that Aristotelian philosophy provides a much needed ethical foundation for the environmental sciences and for our daily commitment to practices of sustainability. Shearman challenges previously held interpretations of Aristotle's value to the grounding of environmental ethics"-- Provided by publisher.
Identifiers: LCCN 2019040356 (print) | LCCN 2019040357 (ebook) | ISBN 9781939125620 (paperback) | ISBN 9781939125637 (ebook)
Subjects: LCSH: Aristotle.
Classification: LCC B485 .S53 2019 (print) | LCC B485 (ebook) | DDC 185--dc23
LC record available at https://lccn.loc.gov/2019040356
LC ebook record available at https://lccn.loc.gov/2019040357

To Suzy

ACKNOWLEDGMENTS

This book represents the culmination of my thinking on the philosophical implications of sustainability and the environmental sciences that have evolved over the past 30 plus years. It may never have seen the light of day were it not for Ralph Sanders, my graduate advisor at the State University of New York, College of Environmental Science and Forestry. Ralph was always there for guidance, advice, or just to chat. I am especially thankful for his unwavering support as I made the difficult transition from scientific to philosophical research--and thus to this specific endeavor.

I also owe much to Caroline Snyder from the Rochester Institute of Technology. She not only was instrumental in hiring me within the Science, Technology, Society Department, but was invaluable as a mentor. She continues to be the very personification of interdisciplinarity.

Laura Westra was also of great help to me at the beginning of my academic career. She gave me confidence that my work on Aristotle had merit and was worth pursuing. She too, has been the embodiment of interdisciplinarity - providing a model of how to think about and address environmental problems and sustainability. It is difficult to articulate how grateful I am for the support she provided.

Finally, I would like to express my deepest thanks to all the good people at RIT Press who played a role in bringing this book to fruition - in particular Bruce Austin and Molly Cort. They not only gave me the opportunity to publish my ideas, but made the process downright enjoyable with their professionalism and personable approach.

TABLE OF CONTENTS

INTRODUCTION

This book aims to introduce students of the environmental sciences to philosophical thinking from within an Aristotelian perspective.[1] The justification for this project emerges from my belief that philosophical reflection should be an important practical and curricular component of applied disciplines – perhaps especially those attempting to address the challenges posed by humanity's current and profoundly unsustainable development path. With its focus on problem-solving, environmental science is necessarily confronted with an assortment of moral questions that emerge from the problem-solving process. These questions can be quite diverse and expansive – ranging from efforts to preserve biodiversity to the realization of environmental justice. At base, and as defined within these pages, environmental science can be understood as a collection of related disciplines seeking to help bring about a better (i.e. sustainable) and more just existence on a resource-limited planet. And yet, with few exceptions,[2] you would be hard pressed to find substantive attention being brought to bear on important baseline moral questions associated with a sustainable vision of the future. Until environmental science actively engages such questions, I fear

---

1 I will use the term environmental science to refer to the various applied environmental problem-solving disciplines such as environmental studies, sustainability science, conservation biology and environmental science unless noted otherwise.

2 Conservation biology stands out among the environmental sciences in that it has sought, from its inception, to justify conserving biodiversity in moral terms. I have more to say on this in the final chapter.

it will lack a clearly defined identity and purpose - an untenable situation for any applied field.

I examine the philosophical/ethical questions associated with environmental problems through an Aristotelian lens for two distinct reasons. First, although there has emerged a fairly robust discussion within the environmental ethics literature drawing upon an Aristotelian conception of human virtue, to my knowledge no one has attempted to develop a more thorough-going Aristotelian response to the philosophical questions associated with environmental sustainability. In other words, beyond an analysis of how virtue ethics can be applied to environmental decision-making, little if any comprehensive attention has been devoted to the other elements of Aristotle's extraordinarily rich philosophical works - such as his conception of the common good, self-love, or metaphysics. Second, I think an Aristotelian approach is particularly well-suited to addressing environmental questions, given the emphasis Aristotle places on biological studies. Upon my reading, Aristotle maintained a reasonably sophisticated ecological worldview that shaped much of his thinking, including his political and moral treatises.[3] If this much is true, then Aristotle should be able to provide a cogent example of how environmental questions can be approached philosophically, and, one would hope, provide a means for non-philosophers to enter the ongoing discussion of "how ought we to live on this earth?"

Chapter 1 begins by offering a synopsis of how Aristotle has been utilized or interpreted within the still relatively new field of

3 Specifically, his *Politics* and *Nicomachean Ethics*.

environmental philosophy. The bulk of the chapter, however, seeks to defend an Aristotelian approach to environmental philosophy against claims that Aristotle's perspective either is incompatible with a concern for the conservation of nature, or shares an important measure of responsibility for attitudes producing the environmental problems we experience today (possibly impeding or dissuading other scholars from engaging in a broad-based examination of Aristotelian thought within environmental philosophy). The argument asserting the antipathy of the Aristotelian tradition toward environmental protection originates in a noncontextualized interpretation of Aristotle's teleology found in I.8 of his *Politics*. While considering issues in household management, Aristotle states that the purpose of plants and animals can be defined in terms of meeting human need or desire. For some scholars, this is evidence that Aristotle envisioned a hierarchical structure to the world with human beings occupying the pinnacle of creation with little or no regard accorded the rest of nature beyond need satisfaction. Those scholars ultimately conclude that Aristotle was incapable of developing an ecological perspective and thus an environmental ethic. However, I will argue that once *Politics* I.8 is placed in context, this profoundly anthropocentric interpretation of Aristotle's position on the relationship of human beings to the rest of the natural world becomes quite tenuous, if not unsupportable. Chapter 1 concludes by arguing that the Aristotelian tradition offers an intellectually stimulating resource from which to reflect on the morality of sustainability, and should be of interest to those of us trying to gain greater conceptual clarity of sustainability as both goal and process.

Chapter 2 attempts to illuminate the structure of Aristotle's moral philosophy. Upon my reading, Aristotle identifies a single grand end consistent with human nature that represents the best life toward which we should aim. Although Aristotle may have identified a single intellectual goal as the object of desire, there are actually many ways to achieve at least a modicum of happiness - all of which are compatible with, or may demand, environmental sustainability. Chapter 3 addresses issues in Aristotle's metaphysics relating to a contemplative life, and the importance of encountering and studying the natural world as a component of human virtue. This emerges from Aristotle's seminal statement "all men by nature desire to know". It is through the active and empirical investigation of the natural world that we can begin to fulfill our desire to understand and thus participate in a way of life that is most complete and blessed. Chapter 4 explores the contextual nature of Aristotle's moral philosophy in greater depth and seeks to explain the significance of this for developing environmental concern. In chapter 5, I draw on Aristotle's ideas about friendship to speculate on the possibility of valuing other forms of life for their own sake in a manner similar to the bond shared among friends. This will provide an argument for all life having inherent value, and thus not dependent upon human valuation. Chapter 6 provides a summary statement of an Aristotelian approach to the issues related to ecological sustainability and its potential relevance to contemporary life.

The final chapter brings us back to my ultimate purpose in writing this book - to argue why moral analysis should be a foundational component of environmental science and its curricula. I contend that the connection between morality and environmental policy formation should be made much more explicit if only as a reminder of our purpose in making policy and thus of what we are seeking to achieve--a better world (or at the very least a viable world) based upon a set of values which define what constitutes "better". In my judgment, ignoring the moral dimensions of policy development and analysis (or pushing them to the periphery of the discipline) invites a superficial assessment of our motivations and goals for policy, and may unnecessarily limit or obscure our response to a given problem. Without acknowledging our moral compass, we may also become so enamored of technical methodology as to mistake means for ends, or calculation for deliberation. This is not to say that the policy-making process will become easier. On the contrary, it may become much more difficult. Yet the purpose of addressing the underlying moral component of policy in environmental science is not to make the process simpler, but rather to make it more comprehensive and effective.

My motivation for addressing these questions emerged in graduate school while studying biology and then environmental science. I have always been sensitive to environmental problems, and thought I could best contribute to their solutions through scientific endeavors. However, as I commenced my doctorate in environmental science, I started to wonder why I cared. This did not reflect a growing callousness to environmental concerns on my part, but simply an inability to offer a lucid argument supporting environmental protection. I knew it was a good thing and wanted to contribute to the cause, but I could not clearly explain why it was right or why I should act. Not being able to answer such a basic question was unsettling and I soon found it impossible to engage in any further scientific work before being able to formulate an adequate response to the question, "why do I care?" and by extension, "why should anyone care?"

Somewhere in my search, I stumbled upon Aristotle. Perhaps it was the attention he paid to biological matters that I found attractive, thus offering me some transitional space between biology and philosophy. Beyond finding in Aristotle an apparent kindred spirit, it was clear to me that he was a keen observer of nature with an ecological view of the world that warranted further study. In the process, I became intrigued with two facets of Aristotle's method that struck me as being necessary for any environmental ethic. First was his moral contextualism. In other words, the good life for Aristotle was something that could not be abstracted from the social and material circumstances of existence. A good human being is one who is able to navigate the many challenges of human existence. As I will try to indicate, Aristotle's moral philosophy is readily adaptable for taking into consideration not only the social conditions of the good life, but the broader environmental conditions as well. Second, Aristotle's moral philosophy is grounded in practical activity, meaning that one must **live** the ethical life within society **and** nature in order to live well. As Lester Brown once noted, "Saving the planet is not a spectator sport."[4] There may well be value in theory development, but environmental science demands that we develop practical solu-

4 Brown, *Launching the Environmental Revolution*, 1992.

tions to "planet saving". Although Aristotle maintains a strong intellectual focus in the *Nicomachean Ethics*, I will endeavor to show that he considered intellectual activity to be constrained by practical reality. At base, the philosophy of Aristotle seemed particularly well suited for any discussion that seeks to define morality within the domain of the natural world.

Another stimulus for this book has been my perception of a diminished appreciation over the years of the importance of ethical analysis as a component of environmental science. This is reflected in a paper by Nelson and Vucetich discussing the impediments to understanding and addressing issues in sustainability from within sustainability science.[5] Lacking an analysis of sustainability as a moral concept, applied sustainability disciplines have essentially become rudderless in their efforts to address environmental problems, since there is no clearly articulated vision, or the means to develop a vision, of what kind of world sustainability entails. The reasons for this unfortunate situation are not clear to me. Does the reluctance to engage moral questions emerge from the fear that moral analysis is a short step away from advocacy, and thus a possible threat to scientific objectivity? Or do elements of positivism pervade the environmental sciences with practitioners questioning, a priori, the legitimacy of moral analysis as an element of their disciplinary framework? Whatever the explanation, I think we have become good at identifying and explaining environmental problems, but not so good at providing direction toward their solution.

5 Nelson & Vucetich, *Sustainability Science: Ethical Foundations and Emerging Challenges*, 2012.

Lastly, in a very real sense this work can be viewed as that of an outsider. I have written a book that is fundamentally philosophical but have no formal training in philosophy. My investigation into Aristotle began while pursuing a doctorate in environmental science at a university known for scientific research, and continued without the benefit of a philosophical mentor. Therefore, the majority of the volume at hand is the result of a personal and substantially auto-didactical intellectual journey into a research tradition that I joined late in my educational career. Yet I see this work as being fundamentally a derivative of environmental science. Since the purpose of environmental science is to seek solutions to environmental problems within an interdisciplinary structure, then any area of research that can assist our efforts to improve environmental conditions should be welcomed under the environmental science banner. Arguably, the starting point for any such endeavor is "why care about environmental sustainability"?

Author Note: The translation I used for the various Aristotelian texts was provided by *The Complete Works of Aristotle*, by Jonathan Barnes.[6] If you decide to read Aristotle yourself, be aware that translators (including Barnes) make use of Bekker numbers. This provides a means to reference a particular text within a given book or chapter by page number, column ("a" or "b"), and line number of the edition first published by the German scholar Immanuel Bekker in 1831. The advantage of this system is that it allows precise ref-

6 Barnes, *The Complete Works of Aristotle*, 1984.

erencing of Aristotle's work, irrespective of any modern translation being used.

NOTES

Jonathan Barnes, *The Complete Works of Aristotle*. (Princeton: Princeton University Press, 1984)

Lester R. Brown, "Launching the Environmental Revolution," in *State of the World 1992*, ed. Linda Starke (New York: Worldwatch Institute, 1992) 174-190.

M.P. Nelson and J.A. Vucetich, "Sustainability Science: Ethical Foundations and Emerging Challenges." *Nature Education Knowledge* 3 (10) (2012): 12.

CHAPTER 1: ARISTOTLE AND ENVIRONMENTAL CONCERN

INTRODUCTION

Aristotle has been the subject of extensive scholarship that continues to the present day, including the effort to extend philosophical thinking to issues arising from modern environmental problems. That said, the perceived value of an Aristotelian approach to addressing issues of environmental concern has been ambiguous. On the one hand, there has emerged much activity among environmental philosophers exploring the relevance of Aristotle's conception of virtue as part of virtue ethics.[1] On the other hand, several environmental philosophers have concluded that the Aristotelian tradition is unsuitable for fostering environmental protection. It has even been suggested that our modern environmental problems can be traced to the emergence of Western attitudes having their roots in Aristotelian philosophy. A potential explanation for this dichotomy is to acknowledge the ubiquity of virtue language within environmental discourse.[2] Since Aristotle has shaped much of our thinking about human virtue, environmental philosophers have often drawn

1 Virtue ethics is considered one of the three major approaches to normative ethics, the other two being deontological and consequentialist ethics. Each provides a distinct framework to assess moral activity. Virtue ethics places emphasis on the development of character traits consistent with being a good person (e.g. honor, honesty, etc.). Deontology emphasizes adhering to defensible duties or rules to guide moral behavior (e.g. treat others as you would have them treat you), and consequentialism emphasizes acting in ways that maximize the well-being of those that matter (e.g. the good of the many over that of the few).

2 Sandler, *Environmental Virtue Ethics*, 2013.

from this important element of his normative philosophy, without committing themselves to accepting everything Aristotelian.

My primary purpose in this chapter is to call into question the assumption that Aristotelian thought is at odds with environmental protection, or has contributed to Western attitudes associated with environmental degradation as embodied in the dominion thesis. While the insights derived from virtue ethics are quite valuable, I think Aristotle has much more to offer us modern folk with respect to finding our place in nature, and why we have good reason to maintain, if not enhance, environmental integrity. To demonstrate the legitimacy of a more broad-based Aristotelian approach to environmental issues, it will first be necessary to establish that the perception among early environmental philosophers that Aristotelian thought is strongly anthropocentric, and thus incompatible with environmental protection, can be traced to a misinterpretation of Aristotle's teleology, and should be rejected.

THE VIRTUE AND VICE OF ARISTOTLE

Barnes characterized Aristotle as a "thunderingly good" philosopher.[3] A considerable portion of his exceptionally diverse writings may be difficult to parse, but they nonetheless offer a rich and satisfying philosophical resource that continues to stimulate a great deal of scholarship to the present day. Currently, the majority of research on Aristotelian approaches to environmental philosophy can be found within the discourse on normative ethics, specifically as it

3 Barnes, *The Cambridge Companion to Aristotle*, 1995, xv.

relates to virtue ethics. According to Sandler,[4] the core questions of environmental virtue ethics are:

1. What makes a character trait an environmental virtue or environmental vice, and which particular character traits (i.e., attitudes and dispositions) are environmental virtues and which are environmental vices? That is, what are the character norms of environmental ethics?
2. What is the role of environmental virtue ethics (or an ethic of character) within environmental ethics?

Given that virtue ethics represents one of the three main pillars of normative ethics and that Aristotle was instrumental in shaping the concept of virtue, then his influence on this field should come as no surprise. The robustness of virtue ethics can be appreciated by noting the many recent publications on the subject.[5]

However, attempts to peer at environmental questions through a more comprehensive Aristotelian lens is quite uncommon among modern philosophers. I find this largely unfilled intellectual space to be rather perplexing given the empirical content of much of Aristotle's work, and his effort to situate human beings within nature. At first glance, and as part of the effort to provide a foundation for the relatively new discipline of environmental philosophy, the Aristotelian tradition would appear to be a fertile philosophical field to plow. Yet, other than what can be found in virtue ethics, there has been limited interest in exploring Aristotelian concepts as applied

4 Sandler, 2013.

5 For a good introduction to virtue ethics complete with an extensive bibliography, see Hursthouse and Pettigrove, *Virtue Ethics. https://plato.stanford.edu/entries/ethics-virtue*, 2016.

to environmental thinking. What explains this apparent oversight?

One possible clue can be located in efforts to determine the origin of our environmental problems once the modern environmental movement was ushered into existence with the publication of *Silent Spring* by Rachel Carson in 1962. Probably the best-known attempt to determine the decision tree leading to our present situation was Lynn White's *The Historical Roots of Our Ecologic Crisis.*[6] In this seminal paper, White argues that our modern environmental problems can be traced to the marriage of science to technology in medieval Europe within the context of Christian dominion ideology.[7] Thus, science came to be identified with the Baconian creed of wresting knowledge from nature for the sake of exerting our technological power and control over it. This was justified by the human/nature dualism inherent in Christian dominion theory that profoundly alienated human beings from nature, and defined our relationship to it in terms akin to master/slave. As White states:

> Despite Copernicus, all the cosmos rotates around our little globe. Despite Darwin, we are *not*, in our hearts, part of the natural process. We are superior to nature, contemptuous of it, willing to use it for our slightest whim.[8]

In consequence, White argues that we will not make any real progress addressing our "ecologic crisis" until we experience a religious transformation of sorts that redefines our relationship to nature in a

[6] White, 1967.

[7] Specifically, the Latin West as opposed to the Greek East tradition within Christianity.

[8] White, 1967, 1206.

more benign, humble and sustainable way.

White was not alone in attempting to determine how we missed boarding the sustainable lifestyle boat. Merchant, in her book *The Death of Nature: Women, Ecology and the Scientific Revolution,*[9] offered what can arguably be viewed as an extension of White's thesis but emphasizing the transformation from an organic to a mechanistic worldview within science during the enlightenment. Instead of viewing the Earth as being alive and filled with sacred spaces that placed moral constraints on the exploitation of nature, scientific mechanism rendered the Earth into an inert and lifeless thing to be subjugated by humans. This was accompanied by a shift in social structure that enhanced the authority of men at the expense of women (or a shift in power and ideology from the feminine to the masculine in western culture). Addressing environmental problems from this perspective will require a move from the oppressive hierarchical structure found in androcentrism and mechanism to something more egalitarian and sustainability-enhancing - perhaps reclaiming some of the ideas of organicism found in the pre-Christian past.

A third line of inquiry seeking to understand the roots of our current environmental predicament, and one that brings us closer to the question at hand, examined the role played by western philosophy, particularly that of ancient Greece, in providing the philosophical firmament for the uncontrolled exploitation of the natural world. J. Donald Hughes argued that although Aristotle's student Theoph-

---

9 Merchant, 1980.

rastus maintained a perspective that very well may have established the basis for an ecological worldview within philosophy, he was ultimately overshadowed by his mentor's anthropocentric teleology that prevented the development of ecological insights and established a utilitarian attitude justifying the unrepentant exploitation of the natural world. According to Hughes, this attitude is the direct result of Aristotle declaring that the proper end of all other living things was the service of man. Hughes concludes his essay by pondering the environmental double whammy resulting from coupling Aristotelian teleology with the Christian ideology of dominion:

> No more effective combination of ideas to encourage the untrammeled exploitation of the earth's natural resources can possibly be imagined.[10]

This line of reasoning was further elaborated by Eugene Hargrove in *Foundations of Environmental Ethics*.[11] Hargrove argued that Western philosophy has not only been either irrelevant or incompatible with environmental concern, it has been responsible for our emerging environmental problems by providing a collection of ideas and attitudes that served to inhibit the protection and preservation of the environment. Contrary to White, he argued that religion (i.e. Christianity) should not be accused of shepherding in the ecologic crisis, since most of the environmentally offensive ideas had their origins in philosophy. In his view, the impact of the dominion theory in Genesis was relatively benign until it came to be interpreted in

10 Hughes, *Ecology of Ancient Greece*, 1975, 124.

11 Hargrove, 1989.

the light of Aristotle's philosophy, which articulated the idea that "... the purpose of the world was the service of man".[12] Hargrove says that, along with early modern European philosophy, classical Greek philosophy was crucial in shaping our current attitudes toward the environment - attitudes that have greatly inhibited environmental concern and protection.

With respect to classical Greek philosophy, Hargrove states that its environmental insensitivity was a manifestation of three unfortunate characteristics that: 1) prevented the development of an ecological perspective, 2) discouraged the aesthetic apprecia-tion of the natural world, and 3) promoted a conception of reality that suppressed the idea or necessity of environmental protection.[13] Hargrove traces the inability of the ancient Greeks to develop an ecological awareness or an appreciation of beauty in the world to a metaphysical perspective unable to admit that the world of every-day experience was real. Therefore, a bias against the observation of the world as a way to either obtain knowledge or derive aesthetic pleasure became manifest, leading the ancients to ignore the earth-ly objects and processes around them. This, Hargrove reasoned, is the result of a line of inquiry having its origin at the very beginning of classical Greek philosophy, at least since the time of Thales.

Although Hargrove admits that "Of all the major Greek philos-ophers, Aristotle was the only one who came close to approaching

---

[12] Hargrove, 1989, 16.

[13] Ibid., 21.

nature from an ecological perspective",[14] he nevertheless fell short of the mark. Since Aristotle was unable to develop an ecological appreciation of the natural world, he was necessarily precluded from an awareness that makes environmental concern possible. Hargrove offers two primary reasons explaining this regrettable situation. First is a lack of evidence suggesting that Aristotle was ever interested in nature protection, despite his recognition that a great deal of environmental change occurred[15] and the significance he placed on the investigation of nature.[16] Second, and more importantly, was his insistence on there being set purposes in nature that are hierarchically arranged in a static universe with humans at the apex. According to Hargrove,

> Noting that change in nature, particularly biological and botanical nature, usually occurred in specific ways involving specific stages, Aristotle concluded that certain kinds of objects, especially living organisms, existed for particular purposes as part of a design built into nature. The purpose or final cause of the existence of an acorn, for example, is an oak tree. Generalizing still further, he concluded that lower organisms existed for the benefit of higher organisms, and they all could be ranked into an order of being, with humans at the top.[17]

Hargrove affirms this anthropocentric and hierarchical ordering of nature by quoting an important passage from the *Politics* discussing property:

---

[14] Ibid., 24.

[15] *Meteorology* 351a19-353a26 as cited by Hargrove, 1989.

[16] Hargrove quotes Aristotle's *On the Parts of Animals* 640b18-29.

[17] Hargrove, 1989, 25.

> Property, in the sense of bare livelihood, seems to be given by nature herself to all, both when they are first born, and when they are grown up. For some animals bring forth, together with their offspring, so much food as will last until they are able to supply themselves; of this the vermiparous or oviparous animals are an instance; and the viviparous animals have up to a certain supply of food for their young in themselves, which is called milk. In like manner we may infer that, after the birth of animals, plants exist for their sake, and that other animals exist for the sake of man, the tame for use and food, the wild, if not all, at least the greater part of them, for food, and for the provision of clothing and various instruments. Now if nature makes nothing incomplete, and nothing in vain, the inference must be that she has made all animals for the sake of man.[18]

Hargrove interprets this passage as a claim that all other life forms were put here for the benefit of humans. Further, since the entire hierarchy is thought permanent and unchanging, an awareness of environmental problems and thus the need for environmental protection was not possible. Finally, Hargrove ventures that in order for Aristotle to achieve a conservation-inducing ecological perspective, he would probably need to abandon his teleology.

Thus, with respect to the question of why Aristotle has had a limited positive impact on modern environmental philosophy beyond what can be found in virtue ethics, it would appear that a prejudice emerged against Aristotle as a consequence of Aristotelian philosophy being deemed largely responsible for creating the mess we must presently endure. However, as I will attempt to demonstrate in the remainder of this chapter, the interpretation of Aristotle's teleology presented by scholars like Hughes and Hargrove

18 *Politics* I, 1256b7-22.

obscures more than it illuminates.[19] In particular, the section of the *Politics* quoted to exemplify Aristotle's teleology and establish his inability to derive a philosophical basis for environmental protection has been taken out of context, and diverts us from appreciating the potential value of an Aristotelian environmental vision. In the following, I will attempt to explain why *Politics I* is not a metaphysical statement and thus not the fundamentally anthropocentric and ecological-awareness-eschewing bugaboo being ascribed to it. In addition, I will try to illustrate how an Aristotelian perspective may actually be quite fruitful in efforts to determine the moral basis for living in a resource-limited world.

ARISTOTLE AND ECOLOGICAL AWARENESS

Contrary to previous scholars like Zeller,[20] and drawing upon a single passage in the *Politics* discussing household management, Hughes claimed that Aristotle considered the purpose of plants and animals to be the satisfaction of human need as part of a natural hierarchy that effectively sanctioned unconstrained environmental exploitation.[21] Hargrove developed this thesis further in his important book *Foundations of Environmental Ethics*.[22] If I understand him correctly, Hargrove insists that ecological awareness is a necessary

---

[19] Attfield, *Has the History of Philosophy Ruined the Environment?* provides a broader critique of Hargrove's conclusions (and by extension, Hughes') regarding the role of philosophy in inhibiting preservationist attitudes.

[20] Costelloe & Muirhead, *Aristotle and the Earlier Peripatetics*, 1897.

[21] Hughes, 1975.

[22] Hargrove, 1989.

precondition for environmental concern. This raises the question of what constitutes ecological awareness? Does it embody a reasonably sophisticated knowledge of how plants, animals, and other living beings interact with each other, and with the abiotic environment, over a determinate time frame? Or can we accept something less stringent, but still recognizably ecological, such as an awareness of dependency or perhaps interdependency within the natural world? In my judgment, the latter is perfectly adequate for eliciting environmental concern among human beings. Although much of ancient Greek philosophy may have caused people to distrust their senses and repress the emergence of what can be described as an ecological awareness, I do not think this can be said of Aristotle.

My defense of Aristotle's capacity for ecological awareness rests in part on an examination of the passage found in *Politics I* that both Hughes and Hargrove reference to demonstrate Aristotle's inherent anthropocentrism and environmental blindness. I will not dispute the premise that Aristotle thought that the cosmos was hierarchically arranged or that, **in the sense described** in the *Politics*, he considered organisms to be for the sake of others and "all animals for the sake of man". The difficulty for the interpretation offered by Hughes and Hargrove rests with their failure to place the passage in context. Upon my reading, Aristotle was not making a grand metaphysical claim about the structure of reality, but rather a practical assessment of the goods necessary or available to make human life possible.

It is important to appreciate that Aristotle is discussing matters of household management in the chapter of the *Politics* at issue. In other words, he is trying to make clear that in order to maintain a household, a manager must acquire the necessary goods (like money, food, and clothing) to satisfy the needs of that household. According to Aristotle, there is an adaptive and dependent relationship among living beings (including human beings) as they seek to secure the resources needed for survival. Given that there are many different kinds of goods available, both humans and other animals exhibit a range of behavior in their acquisition:

> Again, there are many sorts of food, and therefore there are many kinds of lives both of animals and men; they must all have food, and the differences in their food have made differences in their ways of life. For of beasts, some are gregarious, others are solitary; they live in the way which is best adapted to sustain them, accordingly as they are carnivorous or herbivorous or omnivorous: and their habits are determined for them by nature with regard to their ease and choice of food. But the same things are not naturally pleasant to all of them; and therefore the lives of carnivorous or herbivorous animals further differ among themselves. In the lives of men too there is a great difference.[23]

At base, Aristotle is stating the empirical reality that all living things (including humans) must have food in order to persist. An important difference between humans and other animals is that we are not limited by instinct, and can engage in activities that go beyond what is needed for mere survival. Our lives are subject to greater complexities, and may require many different kinds of goods provided by nature.[24] Since Aristotle believed that nature "makes nothing in-

---

[23] *Politics* I, 1256 a19-30.

[24] It was Aristotle's task in the *Nicomachean Ethics* to determine what was unique to human life in order to understand what constitutes the good human life. For Aristotle, this involves more than activities aimed at survival.

complete, and nothing in vain" he concluded that all components in nature can be used for some purpose or in some way. This is fundamentally different from the claim that the reason for existence of other organisms is to meet our wants or needs. If anything, Aristotle is relating ecological principles of dependency (if not interdependency) and population behavior,[25] and not making the stronger claim that the sole purpose for existence of life on earth is to serve humankind.

Ducharme provides a compelling argument supporting this interpretation as part of his assertion that Aristotle's teleology should not be confused with expressing the dominion thesis.[26] According to Ducharme, natural objects are recognized by Aristotle as having interests and are thus valuable in a way independent of their utility. As he says:

> It is not in the nature of the lamb to be eaten even if it may be for the sake of nourishing humans and other animals.[27]

This is an important distinction to recognize. While it is certainly true that Aristotle envisioned a hierarchical structure to the world filled with purpose and purposeful behavior, we should not confuse the desire of a household manager to meet the needs of a family by

---

25 Note that it would not be inaccurate (unorthodox perhaps) to describe the different ecological trophic levels as being "for the sake of" relationships. For example, plants can be said to exist for the sake of herbivores and herbivores for the sake of carnivores as long as we do not insist that this implies some kind of moral order.

26 Ducharme, *Aristotle and the Dominion of Nature*, 2014.

27 Ibid., 213.

using the resources provided by nature, with the notion that nature has no other value other than as a human resource.[28]

I think the attempt to ascribe to Aristotle a teleological perspective that invokes the ghost of Protagoras is ultimately not defensible. I have found no evidence to indicate that Aristotle actually believed that the world expressed the kind of purposive structure that both Hughes and Hargrove read into the passage on household management quoted from the *Politics*. As Gotthelf[29] says, in describing how things come to be "for the sake of" something else, Aristotle is almost exclusively concerned with the generation and development of organisms, and that his thoughts on these matters are fundamentally empirical in character and not the result of some a priori assumption brought to his study of nature.[30] By saying that things are for the sake of something else, Aristotle is primarily concerned with describing the necessary pre-conditions for achieving the goal or *telos* of a being. All animals need food for the sake of growth and development while human beings have additional needs for the sake of happiness.

The above quote from the *Politics* describing the various strategies or adaptations organisms exhibit in their quest to survive, also casts doubt on the claim by Hargrove that Aristotle was incapable

---

[28] That other living things have interests or a good of their own is addressed more fully in later chapters. For example, see *A General Formula for Happiness* in chapter 2.

[29] Gotthelf, *Aristotle's Conception of Final Causality*, 1976.

[30] Hankinson, *Philosophy of Science* (1995), mentions that Aristotle's teleology can also be interpreted as serving a heuristic purpose.

of perceiving the world ecologically. The descriptions of how different kinds of organisms meet their needs through either herbivory, carnivory or omnivory and that animals can be solitary or social are empirical observations of symbioses, and thus a manifestation of an ecological awareness. Frankly, I would be surprised if Aristotle had not been at least capable of seeing the world around him from an ecological perspective (assuming that he did not).[31] Beyond *Politics* I, 1256 a19-30, there is an intriguing section in his *Metaphysics* on the relationship of God to the world and its order that is also suggestive of an ecological vision:

> We must consider also in which of two ways the nature of the universe contains the good or the highest good, whether as something separate and by itself, or as the order of the parts. Probably in both ways, as an army does. For the good is found both in the order and in the leader, and more in the latter; for he does not depend on the order but it depends on him. *And all things are ordered together somehow, but not all alike - both fishes and fowls and plants; and the world is not such that one thing has nothing to do with another, but they are connected.* For all are ordered together to one end ... all share for the good of the whole (my emphasis).[32]

I understand Aristotle to be saying that the world embodies a well-ordered whole in which all species of things are fundamentally connected, including "both fishes and fowls and plants". The ultimate goodness of the world being derived from the order brought to it by God. Being like the leader of an army, God is foundational

---

31 Wiener, *Of Lice and Men: Aristotle's Biological Treatises* (1990), apparently agrees.

32 *Metaphysics* XII.10, 1075a11-25.

"for he does not depend on the order but it depends on him". This suggests to me that Aristotle's metaphysics was at least amenable to the development of an ecological perspective that could in turn have elicited environmental awareness and thus concern. In fact, the quote above is reminiscent of the holism found in contemporary ecology and environmentalism. I am not suggesting that Aristotle embodies the kind of ecological and holistic perspective common among modern environmentalists, but I do not think such a perspective is precluded by his metaphysics. This is illustrated in his biological accounts that seek to explain the growth and development of organisms. According to Aristotle, we cannot make sense of organisms by referring only to their material components - there must be some additional principal present (i.e. form) that can organize the disparate parts into a functional whole. Although Aristotle was preoccupied with studying the structure and form of discrete organisms, the quote above from the *Metaphysics* suggests this principal may be binding at a scale encompassing the whole of life.

Building upon his empirical understanding of what is needed for the household manager to ensure survival, Aristotle addresses the broader challenge of living well. An important characteristic of humanity that contributes to our uniqueness among animals is the ability to lead a morally good life. It is in his moral philosophy, particularly the *Nicomachean Ethics*, that we find a treatment of the question, what is the good life for a human being? In this work, we can better appreciate Aristotle's awareness of the importance of the environment for human welfare.

INSTRUMENTAL GOODS

In the *Nicomachean Ethics*, Aristotle discusses the importance of being well equipped with necessary goods in order to live a good life. Like other Greeks of his time, he was greatly concerned with the circumstances of life, and the role they played in either helping or hindering happiness.[33] Having a "good will" or a certain spirit that could be realized independently of one's situation was not sufficient. In order to live a virtuous life, Aristotle reasoned that important pre-conditions must first be addressed:

> ...for it is impossible, or not easy, to do noble acts without the proper equipment. In many actions we use friends and riches and political power as instruments; and there are some things the lack of which takes the lustre from blessedness, as good birth, satisfactory children, beauty; for the man who is very ugly in appearance or ill-born or solitary and childless is hardly happy, and perhaps a man would be still less so if he had thoroughly bad children or friends or had lost good children or friends by death. As we said, then, happiness seems to need this sort of prosperity in addition; for which reason some identify happiness with good fortune, though others identify it with excellence.[34]

Clearly, humans are constrained by circumstances that either hinder or hasten the good life. Good fortune is one of those circumstances since we frequently encounter things that are beyond our control (e.g. our familial circumstances and physical appearance). Thus, fortune's wheel plays an important role in the blessedness we can expect to achieve in our lives. Mercifully, there are other dependent circumstances in life that are within our control (at least for the most

---

33 For example, see Nussbaum, *The Fragility of Goodness*, 1986.

34 *Nicomachean Ethics* I.8, 1099a31-b8.

part) and these things too can contribute to happiness.

The controllable circumstances of particular concern for Aristotle were political, following from his characterization of the human species as a political animal by nature. Consequently, since the individual cannot be abstracted from society, the good life (if it is to be possible at all) must be realized from within the social realm. It is for this reason that Aristotle states that the good life must be answered in reference to political science.[35] Yet Aristotle was also aware that society itself depended upon broader conditions to exist or to perform properly. This becomes evident in Aristotle's description of the evolution of states. Like an organism, a state must pass through various stages of development aimed at needs fulfillment:

> When several villages are united in a single complete community, large enough to be nearly or quite self-sufficing, the state comes into existence, originating in the bare needs of life, and continuing in existence for the sake of a good life.[36]

Although the function of the state was to secure the various goods needed not just for living but for living well, it originates in what Aristotle calls the bare needs of life, or those associated with survival. It is in this context that Aristotle discusses the importance of household management, and makes the comment that nature makes nothing in vain. Whereas the household manager seeks to acquire the various goods supplied by nature for the sake of life as such, the

[35] *Nicomachean Ethics* 1.2, 1094a24-b11.

[36] *Politics* 1.2, 1252b28-30. Later, Aristotle talks about acquiring the basic necessities of life and concludes that "animals exist for the sake of man" as discussed previously.

role of the state is to acquire and provide the resources necessary for the sake of the good life.

We may argue about the capacity of Aristotle to express environmental concern during his lifetime, but I find little in his philosophical corpus to suggest an inherent inability to acknowledge the existence of environmental problems or to recognize their significance in the effort to live well. His moral and political philosophy make clear the importance of external goods provided by nature, fortune, and the state to realize a prosperous life. But Aristotle also makes clear that the value of nature for human happiness is not exhausted by its economic instrumentality. I offer two additional and closely related factors that Aristotle also thinks contribute to human well-being: 1) the beauty to be found in all forms of life and 2) the importance of empirical investigations of the natural world as a component of the best human life.

THE AESTHETIC APPRECIATION AND CONTEMPLATION OF NATURE

In his discussion of aesthetic appreciation among the ancient Greeks, Hargrove does not mention the point of view of Aristotle. Attfield calls him to task on this omission, but his criticism is diminished when he says that although his impression is that there is nothing to discourage the appreciation of natural beauty within Aristotle's philosophy:

> I am unaware of any evidence for his actually experiencing such appreciation (except in the matter of the stars, and, perhaps, of

> personal beauty)....[37]

There is certainly much territory to cover when reading Aristotle's works, but I am nonetheless surprised that both Hargrove and Attfield seem unaware of the joy and beauty that Aristotle found in nature, especially since his regard for the natural world can be found in a passage as evocative as any that I have read. In the second book of *Parts of Animals* he says:

> Having already treated of the celestial world, as far as our conjectures could reach, we proceed to treat of animals, without omitting, to the best of our ability, any member of the kingdom, however ignoble. For if some have no graces to charm the sense, yet nature, which fashioned them, gives amazing pleasure in their study to all who can trace links of causation, and are inclined to philosophy. Indeed, it would be strange if mimic representations of them were attractive, because they disclose the mimetic skill of the painter or sculptor, and the original realities themselves were not more interesting, to all at any rate who have eyes to discern the causes. We therefore must not recoil with childish aversion from the examination of the humbler animals. Every realm of nature is marvelous: and as Heraclitus, when the strangers who came to visit him found him warming himself at the furnace in the kitchen and hesitated to go in, is reported to have bidden them not to be afraid to enter, as even in that kitchen divinities were present, so we should venture on the study of every kind of animal without distaste; for each and all will reveal to us something natural and something beautiful. Absence of haphazard and conduciveness of everything to an end are to be found in nature's works in the highest degree, and the end for which those works are put together and produced is a form of the beautiful.[38]

Thus, we have in the biological works of Aristotle a recognition of the

[37] Attfield, 1991, 130.

[38] *Parts of Animals* II, 645a4-25.

marvelous beauty found in nature and the pleasure to be derived in its study. He does not limit himself to the study and appreciation of only those animals that "charm the sense", but all animals "however ignoble" because in each can be found something beautiful.

An additional reason for distress about environmental degradation, perhaps particularly with respect to the loss of biological diversity, within an Aristotelian perspective. As I will argue in chapter 2, Aristotle held that there were two ways that one could lead a good life. The first was a life lived according to the ethical virtues. The second was a life lived according to the theoretical virtues. It was in the theoretical life that Aristotle thought we realized our fullest potential, and thus lived the best kind of life as human beings. By studying the natural world, we are engaged in an activity that will give us the wisdom to comprehend the "why" of things. As we amass a greater understanding of nature, not only will we come to recognize the world's wonderful character, but we will begin to fulfill our potential as human beings. This is an important point that should not be minimized, because it is only in our scientific encounters with the natural world that it is made intelligible, and by making it intelligible we actualize our fullest potential as natural beings. As Lear[39] puts it, through the study of the natural world we come to satisfy the desire to understand.

Given that Aristotle associated human well-being with an ability to render the world intelligible by inquiring into the development of life through the observation and scientific study of nature, then I

[39] Lear, *The Desire to Understand*, 1988.

think it is evident why a degraded world could generate significant concern. By diminishing our ability to encounter the variety of species to be found on Earth living according to their nature, we are diminishing our ability to understand the world, and thus to achieve happiness. The only significant weakness of Aristotle's philosophy that I can determine in this regard derives from his belief that the form of each species was eternal.[40] Yet I do not think that this in itself need have prohibited environmental concern among those maintaining an Aristotelian world view. It certainly makes it difficult to consider the possibility that species could be wiped from existence, but there is a difference between considering ultimate reality to be permanent, and being concerned about living the good life in the changeable and perishable world of everyday experience. Belief in the former does not necessarily translate into moral ambiguity in the latter, since there are many threats to human happiness that are not ultimately traced to the extinction of species. Nor does this necessarily undermine the kind of analysis and study characteristic of ecology, given that ecology is not strictly dependent upon the processes of speciation or extinction for its integrity.[41] Surely there remains much left of ecological and moral significance in this world relating to environmental problems that are not unduly constrained by evolutionary events.

40 According to Lear, "Each species-form is eternal, and Aristotle thinks that each individual organism, by realizing its form, participates to the best of its ability in something that is ontologically basic and divine." (p. 275).

41 I do not want to underestimate the importance of evolutionary theory and evolutionary processes for ecology. My only point is that there remains much theoretical content that can be derived from more modest time-scale phenomena.

To illustrate how environmental concern could be generated despite a belief in the ultimate indestructibility of species, consider the following scenario. Let us say that a follower of Aristotle is attempting to lead his life according to theoretical virtue in order to live a good and honorable life. Let us also say that our follower seeks to engage in the kind of biological studies that Aristotle himself undertook as part of his own effort to live virtuously, and that he chooses as his subject of study an organism whose behavior can only be observed in the wild, or at least away from the hubbub of Athens. Knowing that success in his attempt to realize his goal of living well is dependent upon active encounters with representatives of the species in question as a subject of scientific study (for how does one acquire knowledge except through empirical investigation?), our virtuous student embarks on a program of biological field studies.

Although our prospective scholar may not be ready to accept the likelihood that a species could be rendered absolutely extinct, he should have no difficulty in recognizing the possibility of localized extirpation. Such a situation can and has occurred in those instances in which a species or group of species is intolerant of conditions that can result as a consequence of human activities (e.g. farming and logging). In these situations, members of a susceptible species would either migrate to more hospitable areas or perish. Depending upon the level of habitat alteration, the ability of our student to succeed in studying these kinds of sensitive species would be proportionately constrained. The overall impact of this is that some species can and do become less accessible for scientific study, and thus our attempts to understand them either as objects inherently interesting in themselves, or as part of the natural world taken as a whole, would be artificially limited. Given the empiricism of an Aristotelian worldview, I think it probable that this kind of problem would be recognized as a threat to happiness by foreclosing on the opportunity of people to engage in the scientific investigation of species.[42]

ARISTOTLE AND ANTHOPOCENTRISM

As alluded to earlier, Hughes and Hargrove's reading of the portion of the *Politics* dealing with household management led them to claim that Aristotle thought that the purpose of the world was defined in terms of human utility, such that "lower organisms existed for the benefit of higher organisms, and they all could be ranked into an order of being, with humans at the top". As best I can determine, Aristotle is arguing from a theocentric, not anthropocentric perspective. For example, in a discussion of the Soul, Aristotle states that all living things (including humans) strive to participate in the divine insofar as they are able. The basic message Aristotle conveys is that the world is ultimately dependent upon God; that life itself can be seen as a response to God, or as an expression of desire for

42 I am aware that some species are naturally rare, and thus the ability to acquire a scientific understanding of them may be inherently more difficult than for those that are more widely distributed. My point is that human beings can artificially and negatively change population dynamics of various species, whether intentionally or not. Thus, the cause of any limitation to the theoretical understanding of nature as a consequence of human activity would be due to circumstances that are normally controllable. Finding nothing in the philosophy of Aristotle prohibiting the appreciation of an event like local extinction (which could well have occurred in ancient Greece), I do not think it unreasonable to conclude that such an event could have been perceived as an impediment for human happiness, and therefore a political failure, since one must encounter nature in order to understand it.

God.[43] This response can be conveyed at different levels, the most primitive being reproduction and nutrition:

> It follows that first of all we must treat of nutrition and reproduction, for the nutritive soul is found along with all the others and is the most primitive and widely distributed power of soul, being indeed that one in virtue of which all are said to have life. The acts in which it manifests itself are reproduction and the use of food because for any living thing that has reached its normal development and which is unmutilated, and whose mode of generation is not spontaneous, the most natural act is the production of another like itself, an animal producing an animal, a plant a plant, in order that, as far as its nature allows, it may partake in the eternal and divine. *That is the goal towards which all things strive, that for the sake of which they do whatsoever their nature renders possible*[44] (my emphasis).

Since living beings are perishable and cannot live forever, the only way they can participate in the eternal life of the unmoved mover is to reproduce their kind. In other words, whereas individual organisms are mortal, the species-form is everlasting. It is participation in the eternal that is ultimately "for the sake of which" all else is done. Plants and animals need food for the sake of survival, for the sake of reproduction, for the sake of participation in the eternal life of God.

With respect to the place of human beings in the scheme of things, Aristotle's view is made quite clear in a passage of the *Nicomachean Ethics* while distinguishing between practical and theoretical wisdom:

> For it would be strange to think that the art of politics, or practical

43 See section 6.7 in Lear, 1988.

44 *On the Soul* II, 415a24-b1

> wisdom, is the best knowledge, since man is not the best thing in the world ... But if the argument be that man is the best of the animals, this makes no difference; for there are other things much more divine in their nature even than man, e.g., most conspicuously, the bodies of which the heavens are framed.[45]

It is evident in this section that Aristotle did not consider humans to be the pinnacle of existence. I think it true that he thought that humans were superior (or at least potentially so) to the other animals for various reasons, but even then, he was not committed to considering the value of other forms of life strictly in terms of their usefulness to humans.[46] Thus, to say that other species exist for the sake of human beings, and are ordered in such a way that human beings are on the top rung of a Great Chain of Being (as both Hughes and Hargrove interpret Aristotle to be saying) is to miss, on my reading, an essential component of Aristotle's philosophy.[47]

Finally, as mentioned earlier, Hargrove thought that in order for Aristotle to develop an ecological perspective and thus environmental concern, he would minimally have had to abandon his teleology. But given that Aristotle's explicit and/or implicit concern for environmental integrity is actually generated from his teleological assumptions, then this suggestion is not reasonable.

---

45 *Nicomachean Ethics* VI.7, 1141a20-b1.

46 In *Nicomachean Ethics* VI.7, 1141a20-b9, Aristotle states that animal species have a good of their own. This indicates the possibility of attributing to other species of life a non-anthropocentric form of value as Ducharme claimed. I develop this further in Chapter 5.

47 This is why I find perplexing the notion that Aristotle's student Theophrastus came to reject "the Aristotelian doctrine that animals, plants, and the earth existed solely for the sake of man." Hargrove, 1988, 26.

CONCLUSION

Outside of virtue ethics, I have found little in the literature seeking to apply Aristotelian principles to the problems of sustainability. This state may be the result of the assumption among some environmental philosophers that Aristotle's teleology is strongly anthropocentric and ultimately incapable of generating environmental concern. Hughes went so far as to accuse Aristotelian philosophy (together with Christian dominion theory) as being an enabler of attitudes and behaviors that have culminated in our "ecological crisis". So not only has Aristotelian thought been judged by some scholars to be woefully inadequate as a guide for environmentalists, it has actually been a causal factor of environmental degradation and is therefore part of the problem!

Although I do not think that anthropocentrism necessarily precludes the development of attitudes favoring the protection of the natural world (consider the conservationism of Gifford Pinchot), it is nonetheless clear to me that Aristotle does not articulate a fundamentally anthropocentric teleology ascribed to him by researchers like Hughes and Hargrove since he does not maintain that all other living beings exist strictly for the sake of human beings.[48] Further, having reviewed much of the Aristotelian corpus including the oft-quoted (and noncontextualized) passage in *Politics* I.8 used to

48 I say "fundamentally anthropocentric" because one can argue that Aristotle's teleology is anthropocentric given the attention paid to human well-being despite the important role played by god. For example, Sedley, *Is Aristotle's Teleology Anthropocentric?* says "Nature is anthropocentric to the extent man is the ultimate beneficiary, while god remains the ultimate object of aspiration, that which all lesser beings strive to imitate." 1991, 180.

prove Aristotle's essential unsuitability for environmental thinking, it is my opinion that not only can the philosophy of Aristotle generate concern for the natural world, it can do so in a way that is quite engaging and stimulating. I maintain that Aristotle was at the very least minimally cognizant of fundamental ecological relationships, since he clearly recognized the dependency of living things (including humans) upon the larger natural world - an important prerequisite for fostering environmental concern. In fact, I think there is every reason to believe that Aristotle would have been greatly distressed at the possibility of environmental destruction had it been evident. This is plainly implied by the importance he places on being adequately equipped with external goods, including those supplied by Nature, and the value he places on the aesthetic appreciation and contemplation of the Natural world. Thus, if western society has been slow to develop an environmental awareness, I don't think the Aristotelian tradition is to blame.

NOTES

Robin Attfield, "Has the History of Philosophy Ruined the Environment?" *Environmental Ethics* 13 (2)(1991): 127-137.

Jonathan Barnes, *The Cambridge Companion to Aristotle* (New York: Cambridge University Press, 1995)

The Complete Works of Aristotle. (Princeton: Princeton University Press, 1984)

B.F.C. Costelloe and J.H. Muirhead, *Aristotle and the Earlier Peripatetics* (New York, NY: Longmans, Green, and Co.,1897)

Alain Ducharme, "Aristotle and the Dominion of Nature." *Environmental Ethics* 36 (2)(2014): 203-214.

Allan Gotthelf, "Aristotle's Conception of Final Causality." *The Review of Metaphysics* (Philosophy Education Society Inc.) 30 (2)(1976): 226-254.

R.J. Hankinson, "Philosophy of Science." In *The Cambridge Companion to Aristotle* by Jonathan Barnes, 109-139. (New York: Oxford University Press,1995).

Eugene C. Hargrove, *Foundations of Environmental Ethics* (Englewood Cliffs: Prentice-Hall, 1989).

Donald J. Hughes, "Ecology of Ancient Greece." *Inquiry* 18 (1975): 115-125.

Rosalind Hursthouse and Glen Pettigrove, "Virtue Ethics" *The Stanford Encyclopedia of Philosophy*,ed. Edward N. Zalta Winter (2016). https://plato.stanford.edu/entries/ethics-virtue/.

Jonathan Lear, *Aristotle: The Desire to Understand.* (New York: Cambridge University Press, 1988).

Carolyn Merchant, *The Death of Nature: Women, Ecology, and the Scientific Revolution* (New York: HarperCollins, 1980).

Martha Nussbaum, *The Fragility of Goodness: Luck and Ethics in Greek Tragedy and Philosophy* (New York: Cambridge University Press, 1986).

Ronald Sandler, "Environmental Virtue Ethics," in *The International Encyclopedia of Ethics*, by Hugh LaFollette (Blackwell Publishing Ltd., 2013), 1665-1674.

David Sedley, "Is Aristotle's Teleology Anthropocentric?" *Phronesis* 36 (2)(1991): 179-196.

L. Weiner, "Of Lice and Men: Aristotles Biological Treatises." *The St. John's Review* 40 (1)(1990): 39-52.

Lynn White, "The Historical Roots of Our Ecologic Crisis." *Science* 155 (3767)(1967): 1203-1207.

CHAPTER 2: A GOOD AND THE BEST LIFE

INTRODUCTION

In this chapter I shall examine the moral philosophy of Aristotle in order to provide a deeper appreciation of what he considered to be a good life.[1] In the process, I aim to provide greater support for my assertion that Aristotle's philosophy is far from incapable of generating environmental concern, as both Hughes and Hargrove argued. A potential impediment to my analysis is a disagreement on how Aristotle defined the structure of the good life. Ackrill argues that Aristotle's idea of individual happiness embodies a **composite** of various intrinsic goods.[2] This is to say that a good person will be one who can accommodate the various things or activities deemed important for living well without giving undue attention to any one thing or activity. On the other hand, Kraut[3] claims that Aristotle identifies the good life with but one type of good (i.e. excellent activity of the rational soul). Thus, a good person will structure his or her life in accordance with this **single good** and subordinate all other goods for its sake. These distinct positions find that the *Nicomachean Ethics* as a whole is either inconsistent (Ackrill) or consistent (Kraut) with respect to the conception of happiness. I personally find the reasoning of Kraut and the idea of a "Grand End" as it re-

1 Aristotle deemed both politics and ethics to be components of moral philosophy. Of his ethical writings, the *Nicomachean Ethics* is thought to represent his most mature statement on morality.

2 Ackrill, *Aristotle on Eudaimonia*, 1980.

3 Kraut, *Aristotle on the Human Good*, 1989.

lates to moral behavior to be the most compelling and consistent with my own reading of the *Nicomachean Ethics.*

That being the case, I will attempt to explain how Aristotle's single good is capable of generating multiple paths to happiness along a continuum that originates from a bipartite conception of living well. This is followed by an examination of the importance Aristotle places upon determining the function of human beings as part of his conception of happiness. Once the function of human beings is determined, then it becomes evident why Aristotle emphasized collective versus individual happiness. Finally, I consider the overall structure of Aristotle's ethical thinking, and argue that it can best be understood as embodying a hierarchy of ends subordinated by a single supreme end that can only be accommodated within political society as situated within the broader environment. An important consequence of this line of enquiry is to call into question the idea that human beings are inherently superior, simply by being human, to other living things.

IDENTIFYING THE GOOD LIFE

Aristotle begins the *Nicomachean Ethics* by saying that all things are thought to aim at some good. He then speculates that if there is something at which all things aim and is desired for its own sake and not for the sake of anything further (otherwise the process would be infinite), then this must be the chief good. Assuming this is true, he adds, "Will not the knowledge of it, then, have a great influence on life? Shall we not, like archers who have a mark to aim at, be more likely to hit upon what we should?".[4] Aristotle goes on to say that if this much can be accepted then it would be worth the effort to both determine this good and the sciences or capacities associated with its study. Thus, at the outset, Aristotle is making clear that the object of his inquiry is a determination of the highest good in human life that gives structure and order to all that we do.[5]

To clarify his position, Aristotle notes the general agreement that this best of all goods is called happiness and that happiness has in turn been identified with living well. To the question of what is meant by happiness, Aristotle says that most men identify it with pleasure, since so many occupy themselves with the life of enjoyment. Contrary to this common opinion, Aristotle concludes in X 7-8 that two kinds of lives can justifiably be said to be happy (although not equally so): the political and contemplative lives respectively. The first and best kind of life is one that involves contemplative activity. The second-best kind of life is one that involves political or practical activity. Each share in common an activity of the reasoning part of the soul that seeks to grasp a body of truths that are either eternal (the objects of contemplation) or variable (the objects of practical deliberation):

> ... since moral excellence is a state concerned with choice, and choice is deliberate desire, therefore both the reasoning must be true and the desire right, if the choice is to be good, and the latter must pursue just what the former asserts. Now this kind of intellect and of truth is practical; of the intellect which is con-

4 *Nicomachean Ethics* I.2, 1094a22-5.

5 Assuming such a good exists. Thus far, Aristotle is only committed to the hypothetical possibility that what he has said so far is true.

> templative, not practical nor productive, the good and the bad state are truth and falsity (for this is the function of everything intellectual); while of the part which is practical and intellectual the good state is truth in agreement with right desire ... The function of both the intellectual parts, then, is truth.[6]

Although the ultimate function of both intellectual activities is to consider truth, they differ in the type of truth being deliberated. Contemplation involves the grasping of first principles that form the basis of the theoretical disciplines.[7] Practical deliberation involves "truth in agreement with right desire" that form the basis of politics and/or the ethical life.

This is important because Aristotle considered the understanding of basic truths (at least with respect to first principles) to be divine.[8] Since we are able to understand the basic truths associated with theoretical and practical knowledge (the function of the intellectual parts of the soul), we have elements within us that are either divine (i.e. our ability to grasp first principles), or a close approximation to the divine (i.e. our ability to make correct choices on practical matters). It is the divine element in the form of our intellect that Aristotle considers the best part of ourselves if not that which defines us most fully, due to its being our natural ruler:

> [intellect] would seem, too, to be each man himself, since it is the authoritative and better part of him. It would be strange, then, if he were to choose not the life of himself but that of something else. And what we said before will apply now; that which

6 *Nicomachean Ethics* VI.2, 1139a22-31 and b11-13.

7 Kraut, 1989, 15.

8 See *Metaphysics* I.2, or XII.7.

> is proper to each thing is by nature best and most pleasant for each thing; for man, therefore, the life according to intellect is best and pleasantest, since intellect more than anything else *is* man.[9]

At base, human beings **are** intellect or understanding. It is the activity of understanding that sets us apart from plants and other animals and ought to determine how we should live.[10] Given that there are two different kinds of intellectual activity aimed at the understanding of truth, then there are two different kinds of lives that can realize happiness or blessedness.

That being said, Aristotle clearly considered the contemplative life to be superior to the practical life, even though each provides an example of living well. The superiority of the contemplative life is derived from its being the closest approximation to the life of God - the model of absolute happiness.[11] For Aristotle, it was not enough simply to live a human life; one should live the best human life possible. Consequently, in order to achieve the greatest level of happiness humanly possible, one ought to strive to live a life that is divine:

> ... it is not insofar as he is man that he will live so, but in so far as something divine is present in him; and by so much as this is superior to our composite nature is its activity superior to that

---

9 *Nicomachean Ethics* X.7, 1178a2-9. Aristotle is referring to the intellect associated with contemplation.

10 As Aristotle says in *Nicomachean Ethics* I.7, 1097b32-1098a1: "Life seems to be common even to plants, but we are seeking what is peculiar to man."

11 As Aristotle says in *Nicomachean Ethics* X.8, 1178b22-24: "...the activity of God, which surpasses all others in blessedness, must be contemplative; and of human activities, therefore, that which is most akin to this must be most of the nature of happiness."

> which is the exercise of the other kind of excellence. If intellect is divine, then, in comparison with man, the life according to it is divine in comparison with human life. But we must not follow those who advise us, being men, to think of human things, and, being mortal, of mortal things, but must, so far as we can, make ourselves immortal, and strain every nerve to live in accordance with the best thing in us; for even if it be small in bulk, much more does it in power and worth surpass everything.[12]

As I understand this passage, Aristotle is emphasizing that our theoretical intellect is the best part of us and represents the divine element within us. Therefore, he can claim that the intellectual activity corresponding to the life of contemplation is superior to that of practical reasoning, given that the former is more divine in comparison to the latter. This leads him to assert that we should strive to the best of our ability to become immortal by engaging in the same activity of the immortal unmoved mover - the standard by which happiness is measured.

In a sense, Aristotle is asking us to transcend our strictly human nature in order to realize our humanity. Given that we are endowed with the innate capacity to render the world intelligible, and thus contemplate first principles as God does, we have the capability of becoming Godlike. Although the life of practical wisdom is considered a good life in that it too involves the exercise of the intellect (but for practical purposes dealing with human matters) it cannot be considered the best life that a human being can lead because it does not partake directly of divine activity. The truths pondered by the practical intellect deal with our lives as mortal beings. Since these truths are variable and not everlasting, a life led in accordance

12 *Nicomachean Ethics* X.7, 1177b27-1178a1.

with them can be happy in only a secondary and transient way:

> But in a secondary degree the life in accordance with the other kind of excellence is happy; for the activities in accordance with this befit our human estate.[13]

Thus, in the attempt to define the best life for a human being in the *Nicomachean Ethics*, Aristotle seems to claim that it is something other than a human life. On the surface this may sound strange, but once we consider the fundamental role played by God in giving structure and order to the cosmos, it becomes less so.

All of this is not to say that the earthly domain of human life is not important. Aristotle was well aware that human life is mortal and perishable and thus depends upon satisfying the various needs that life requires. After stating that happiness must be some form of contemplation, Aristotle immediately adds:

> But, being a man, one will also need external prosperity; for our nature is not self-sufficient for the purpose of contemplation, but our body also must be healthy and must have food and other attention.[14]

Aristotle is here reminding us that we are not gods but mortal beings. By claiming that the best life is one devoted to contemplation, Aristotle is identifying an ideal. If we could spend all of our time contemplating the eternal basic truths, then such a life would be completely happy and blessed. But Aristotle recognized that, as we

13 *Nicomachean Ethics* X.8, 1178a9-10.

14 *Nicomachean Ethics* X.8, 1178b33-35. See also I.8, 1099a31-b8 and I.10, 1101a14-16.

are mortal beings, the contemplative life is more aspirational than achievable for most. Yet we can still have a share in happiness by exercising our intellect with respect to practical affairs. And we *must* pay attention to the practical matters of day-to-day living however much emphasis is placed upon the value of contemplation because, after all, we are perishable beings.

A GENERAL FORMULA FOR HAPPINESS

Another curious element of the *Nicomachean Ethics* is the provision of a general formula for happiness that can be used to compare the relative happiness of all forms of life, not just human life. Although Aristotle is here concerned with what constitutes the good life for human beings, the measure is one that is applicable to all life, including God. In fact, Aristotle makes explicit reference to this in a discussion on the nature of happiness:

> ... the other animals have no share in happiness, being completely deprived of such activity [contemplation]. For while the whole life of the gods is blessed, and that of men too in so far as some likeness of such activity belongs to them, none of the other animals is happy, since they in no way share in contemplation. Happiness extends, then, just so far as contemplation does, and those to whom contemplation more fully belongs are more truly happy, not accidentally, but in virtue of the contemplation; for this is in itself precious.[15]

God "surpasses all others in blessedness" because God does nothing more than contemplate. The rest of life can become happy only to the extent that one engages in contemplation (or secondarily

15 *Nicomachean Ethics* X.8, 1178b24-31.

through successful practical deliberation). Since human beings are the only mortals capable of such activities, then we are the only mortal beings capable of becoming happy. God is used as the measure of happiness because not only is the divine life most blessed, but also because all living things strive to imitate God in order to "... partake in the eternal and divine".[16] That was the basis for my claim in the previous chapter that Aristotle's philosophy is theocentric and not anthropocentric, for he clearly does not consider human beings to be the best of living things or the most blessed. That title is reserved for God, and it is the life of God that all living things seek to emulate insofar as they are able.

To say that nonhuman life in the perishable domain of the biosphere can have no share of happiness is not a claim that their lives are not good, or that they cannot live well in their own way. Aristotle indicates that "even in inferior creatures there is some natural good stronger than themselves which aims at their proper good".[17] A complicating factor in this assessment is that each species has a good specific to itself:

> ... there will be many wisdoms; there will not be one concerned with the good of all animals (any more than there is one art of medicine for all existing things), but a different wisdom about the good of each species.[18]

[16] *On the Soul* II.4, 415a30-b1. See also *Nicomachean Ethics* VII.13, 1153b25-32 and X.2, 1173a4-5.

[17] *Nicomachean Ethics* X.2, 1173a4-5. See also *Parts of Animals* II.10, 656a7-9; *Eudemian Ethics* I.7, 1217a18-29; *Generation of Animals* I.23, 731a30-b3, II.1 731b24-30.

[18] *Nicomachean Ethics* VI.7, 1141a31-33.

As indicated here, all species have a good that is particular to each (as is the case for the human species). This is derived from the idea that all species have a specific function, or a different way of realizing their good in nature, as exhibited by the range of behaviors and strategies employed by the diversity of species to sustain their existence. Further, while there may be no one wisdom "concerned with the good of all animals", all animals have a good of their own, however limited.

What seems evident is that Aristotle envisions a natural and emergent hierarchy that is generated by the single standard of contemplation. The extent to which any creature can be said to live well is measured by the extent it participates in divine activity (i.e. the closer a being is to the life of the divine, the better). If it is the case that a being can actually contemplate the same first principles that God continuously contemplates (as human beings can), then happiness increases in proportion to the level it contemplates throughout its life. The major point of separation between God and other living beings is that God is eternal and completely self-sufficient. In other words, God does not require resources in order to contemplate, for such a being is eternal and in need of nothing external. Aristotle says that human beings too can lead lives that are self-sufficient, but not in the manner of God, since even the most contemplative person will still require the addition of external goods to keep them alive and well. Phrased differently, the most self-sufficient human life is one devoted to contemplation, but given that we are both social and mortal, Aristotle is quick to make clear in I.7 that we cannot live in isolation.[19] We need friends, family, food, and the various other external goods necessary to sustain our lives so that we have the means to engage in contemplation. Significantly, contemplation does not require an excess of wealth beyond what is needed for sustenance. In fact, Aristotle indicates that an excess of wealth may well inhibit contemplative activity.[20] The contemplative life is thus the most self-sufficient life in so far as it demands the least amount of supplemental goods for its exercise.

Although Aristotle stated that there are two kinds of lives that can become happy, I do not take him to mean that there are just two discrete possibilities for leading a happy life. Aristotle's formula appears capable of admitting a range of possible variations of happiness along a continuum. There is thus a basis for making comparisons between and among the lives of different human beings and, if desired, of ranking them according to their relative level of happiness or success. Those who spend more time in contemplation than others lead the best lives, as the amount of contemplation is the sole criterion for determining "complete" happiness. But there is also the possibility of achieving an "incomplete" form of happiness corresponding to the amount of time one spends in excellent practical reasoning. Further, a person can live well by spending a portion

19 In *Nicomachean Ethics* I.7, 1097b8-11 Aristotle says, "Now by self-sufficient we do not mean that which is sufficient for a man by himself, for one who lives a solitary life, but also for parents, children, wife, and in general for his friends and fellow citizens since man is sociable by nature." To this can be added the additional external goods supplied by nature in the form of food and other necessities, for Aristotle was quite aware that in order to live well one must be able to live (see X.8, 1178b33-35).

20 *Nicomachean Ethics* X.8, 1178b4-5.

of his or her time in contemplation and another portion in excellent practical reasoning. As a result, many permutations of happiness are possible corresponding to the relative time one spends in practical and/or contemplative activity. However, the best possible life is one devoted to the most contemplation humanly possible, because one can never become too happy or successful.[21] A minimally happy life is one that actualizes the least amount of excellent practical reasoning.[22] And then there is everything in between.

However, I do not want to leave the impression that Aristotle was concerned with rating lives along some happiness metric. My point is merely that there is within Aristotle's conception of happiness a full range of possible lives that can justifiably be called happy; not that Aristotle is trying to provide a litmus test for comparing those lives. I think what Aristotle is most intent on demonstrating is that if

21 "Happiness extends, then, just so far as contemplation does...", *Nicomachean Ethics* 1178b29. This indicates to me that Aristotle does not put an upper limit on the amount of contemplation that is desirable. As mentioned previously, this does not mean that a person should contemplate continuously and to the exclusion of everything else. Such a life is simply not possible among mortal beings. In addition, we may have obligations to others that compel us to lead a life without happiness, or at a lower level of happiness than might otherwise have been possible. This will be addressed shortly.

22 What minimum period of time must be spent in excellent activity in order to become happy is never stated by Aristotle. All he says is that it must encompass a fairly substantial period for "one swallow does not make a summer, nor does one day; and so too one day, or a short time, does not make a man blessed and happy" (*Nicomachean Ethics* I.7, 1098a18-19). Aristotle makes clear that such precision is not to be expected in any event as, "Our discussion will be adequate if it has as much clearness as the subjectmatter admits of... We must be content, then, in speaking of such subjects and with such premises to indicate the truth roughly and in outline, ... for it is the mark of an educated man to look for precision in each class of things just so far as the nature of the subject admits ..." (*Nicomachean Ethics* I.4, 1094b12-27).

we have a specific target to guide our lives, then that will be of great significance. According to his reasoning, a life that is structured for the sake of contemplation has the correct target in focus and will be more apt to achieve blessedness in its fullest sense.

THE FUNCTION OF HUMAN LIFE

As mentioned previously with respect to species, Aristotle thought that all things were defined by their function. For example, in *Meteorology* Aristotle says:

> What a thing is is always determined by its function: a thing really is itself when it can perform its function; an eye, for instance, when it can see. When a thing cannot do so it is that thing only in name, like a dead eye or one made of stone, just as a wooden saw is no more a saw than one in a picture.[23]

What something is depends on what it does. This is true of all things including humans. Therefore, if we want to find out what human beings are, then we must determine what human beings do. Armed with this information, we can resolve what it is to be a virtuous human being in the sense of fulfilling our function well. As Aristotle says:

> Presumably, however, to say that happiness is the chief good seems a platitude, and a clearer account of what it is is still desired. This might perhaps be given, if we could first ascertain the function of man. For just as for a flute-player, a sculptor, or any artist, and, in general, for all things that have a function or activity, the good and the 'well' is thought to reside in the function, so

[23] *Meteorology* IV.12, 390a10-14. See also *On the Soul* II.1, 412b10-24; *Generation of Animals* I.2, 716a19-26; *Metaphysics* VII.10, 1035b14-17; *Politics* I.2, 1253a22-25.

> would it seem to be for man, if he has a function. Have the carpenter, then, and the tanner certain functions or activities, and has man none? Is he naturally functionless? Or as eye, hand, foot, and in general each of the parts evidently has a function, may one lay it down that man similarly has a function apart from all these? What then can this be?[24]

Aristotle's conception of virtue meant only to do something well, or in an excellent manner, provided that it was not bad or evil. Thus, a virtuous athlete would be one that excelled in some sport or sports. In the same way, Aristotle was concerned with our leading virtuous lives (providing the important distinction between living and living well), as he was convinced that happiness could only be achieved through virtuous activity. This is made clear when he asks:

> Why then should we not say that he is happy who is active in *conformity with complete excellence* and is sufficiently equipped with external goods, not for some chance period but throughout a complete life?[25] (my emphasis).

To lead a happy life is to lead it in accordance with excellence or virtue. But in order to ascertain what constitutes a virtuous human life, it is first necessary to define "a human life" as determined by our function. Consequently, it was of utmost importance to Aristotle to discover our function as human beings in order to determine what it meant to function well. Given that each species had its own function with its own attendant good based upon that function, Aristotle was intent upon finding what was unique to human life in order to differentiate the human good from the good of other animals. As

[24] *Nicomachean Ethics* I.7, 1097b23-32.

[25] *Nicomachean Ethics* I.10, 1101a14-16.

he says in I.7, "Life seems to be common even to plants, but we are seeking what is peculiar to man".[26] It is at this point in book I that Aristotle indicates that the function of human beings "...is an activity of the soul in accordance with, or not without, rational principle".[27] Since a good human being is one who lives an excellent human life, "...human good turns out to be activity of soul in conformity with excellence, and if there are more than one excellence, in conformity with the best and most complete".[28]

Aristotle then postpones further discussion of this particular argument on human function until chapter 6 of Book X, where he once again considers the nature of happiness. Whereas he leaves us with only the hypothetical possibility of there being more than one excellence in I.7, he makes clear in X 7-8 that there are indeed two such excellences associated with the activity of soul in accordance with reason. The first corresponds to our composite nature, or to our mortal existence as a combination of form and matter. The proper excellence for our perishable selves is one aimed at the ethical life based upon what Aristotle calls "right desire". The second corresponds to the divine element of our nature, or to the immortal aspect that underlies our material existence (which is form alone - the subject of chapter 3). The proper excellence for our immortal selves is one aimed at the philosophical life of active contemplation. Given that Aristotle considered the contemplative life to be the proper function of human

26 *Nicomachean Ethics* I.7, 1097b32-1098a1.

27 *Nicomachean Ethics* I.7, 1098a7-8.

28 *Nicomachean Ethics* I.7, 1098a15-16.

beings, and thus the one that most fundamentally defines what it is to be human, he concludes that it should be our ultimate target and for the sake of which all else should be organized. I believe that to be his intention when he speaks of happiness as distinct from "complete" happiness. The ethically virtuous life achieves a subordinate form of happiness, because it is qualitatively less desirable than the divine activity of God. But it does involve a variant of intellectual activity, and at least approximates the most blessed of lives. However, it is not until we actually begin living like God that we can achieve complete happiness or the kind of life that exhibits the most perfect of virtues.[29] But again, although contemplative activity most fully defines who we are, ethical virtue remains a necessary prerequisite for complete happiness given our mortality.

There is one additional point I want to make in this section, and that is that the function of human beings and other living things is an activity. Happiness, therefore, is not an end state or something that results when all the philosophizing or all the practical deliberation has been completed. One does not go about creating happiness as one would an omelet. It is only by engaging in the activity itself (either contemplation or ethical reasoning), that we may attain happiness. Further, it must be an activity that a person engages in for an extended period of time over an entire life for "...one swallow does not make a summer, nor does one day; and so too one day, or a short time, does not make a man blessed and happy". Happiness is thus a way of life and not an end state. It is for this reason that

[29] See Kraut (1989) for a discussion of perfect virtue, particularly the sections on "Complete Virtue" and "Imperfect Virtue" in chapter 4.

Aristotle argues that the aim of the *Nicomachean Ethics* is not to have knowledge of the good life, but rather to become good "...since otherwise our inquiry would have been of no use".[30]

Further, ethical or theoretical activity must take place within the context of society, since human beings are political by nature, and require external support to be successful. That is why Aristotle considers political science to be the most authoritative discipline regarding the human good.[31] But he also makes clear that human happiness is primarily concerned with the collective good, as opposed to the good of the individual in society (although they normally go in one and the same direction). For this reason, Aristotle thinks that the collective good takes priority in times of conflict:

> For even if the end is the same for a single man and for a state, that of the state seems at all events something greater and more complete both to attain and to preserve; for though it is worth while to attain the end merely for one man, it is finer and more godlike to attain it for a nation or for city-states.[32]

The well-being of the state is more godlike than that of the individual because the state is metaphysically prior. This is especially evident in the opening chapters of the *Politics* where Aristotle discusses the development of society:

> Further, the state is by nature clearly prior to the family and to

30 *Nicomachean Ethics* II.2, 1103b28-29.

31 In *Nicomachean Ethics* I.2, 1093a26-9 Aristotle says, "[Happiness] would seem to belong to the most authoritative art and that which is most truly the master art. And politics appears to be of this nature..."

32 *Nicomachean Ethics* I.2, 1094b7-11.

> the individual since the whole is of necessity prior to the part; for example, if the whole body be destroyed, there will be no foot or hand, except homonymously, as we might speak of a stone hand; for when destroyed the hand will be no better than that. But things are defined by their function and power; and we ought not to say that they are the same when they no longer have their proper quality, but only that they are homonymous. The proof that the state is a creation of nature and prior to the individual is that the individual, when isolated, is not self-sufficing; and therefore he is like a part in relation to the whole. But he who is unable to live in society, or who has no need because he is sufficient for himself, must be either a beast or a god: he is no part of a state.[33]

Clearly, Aristotle is here proclaiming the priority of whole to part. The society is prior to the individual because each individual is defined in terms of his or her relationship within society as part to whole. Anyone capable of living in abstraction from external needs (including social interaction) lies outside the functional definition of "human". It is within this context of fulfilling our function as beings capable of intellectual virtue that Aristotle considers human interrelationships.

INDIVIDUAL AND COLLECTIVE HAPPINESS

Provided that Aristotle was primarily concerned with the well-being of the community as a whole, it becomes understandable why he thought politics should serve the common interest. Consequently, any form of government deviating from this goal was considered a perversion of the natural order. Thus, in *Politics* III.7, 1179a28-30

---

[33] *Politics* I.2, 1253a19-30. See also Mulgan, *Aristotle's Political Theory: An Introduction for Students of Political Theory* (1977) for a good discussion on what Aristotle meant by "whole" and "part."

we find that

> The true forms of government, therefore, are those in which the one, or the few, or the many, govern with a view to the common interest; but governments which rule with a view to the private interest, whether of the one, or of the few, or of the many, are perversions.

It is the proper aim of political science to bring about the conditions whereby citizens can be assured of leading happy lives (making it the master art). This makes the end of politics something special and distinctive in that it is concerned with the good life. But in the real world, governments frequently miss the mark by catering to private interests, with the result that they manifest deviant forms of government (e.g. tyranny, oligarchy, or democracy).

It follows from this that Aristotle considered happiness in general to be the proper aim of all people, not necessarily that of private interests (whether of one, few, or many). That is to say that we should act virtuously for the sake of happiness irrespective of the effects this action might have on our personal well-being. In other words, situations may arise which threaten our personal happiness by denying us the opportunity to engage in virtuous activity, at least to the extent that we may have hoped. This could happen by sheer bad luck, or mishap due to circumstances beyond our control.[34] There are other situations, however, that threaten personal happi-

[34] Although Aristotle thought that bad luck need not lead to an unhappy life as a truly good person will always make the best of circumstances, it can nevertheless diminish the blessedness of life. As he says in *Nicomachean Ethics* I.10, 1100a6-7, "... the happy man can never become miserable --though he will not reach blessedness, if he meet with fortunes like those of Priam."

ness **because** one is of good character. For example, when speaking of the virtue of courage, Aristotle discusses how the virtuous man may be compelled to endure hardship and pain, perhaps even to the extent of sacrificing his life in order to do what is noble. In fact, the more virtuous the person who exhibits courage, the more pain he will have to face in moments of crisis:

> And the more he is possessed of excellence in its entirety and the happier he is, the more he will be pained at the thought of death; for life is best worth living for such a man, and he is knowingly losing the greatest goods, and this is painful. But he is none the less brave, and perhaps all the more so, because he chooses noble deeds of war at that cost. It is not the case, then, with all the excellences that the exercise of them is pleasant, except in so far as it reaches its end.[35]

Aristotle is here saying that being virtuous does not guarantee a pleasant or comfortable life. It is certainly a good life if not the best life for a human being to lead, but virtue may still compel one to suffer great pain, and perhaps death for the common good.

To better appreciate this perspective, I think it helpful to recall what Aristotle said at the very beginning of the *Nicomachean Ethics*: all things aim at some good with all other actions being done for the sake of this good. Given that the chief good is happiness, then it is for the sake of this that we structure our lives and base our decisions on the day-to-day matters we encounter throughout life's journey. But he clearly does not mean that the ultimate goal is defined in terms of maximizing personal happiness, since situations may arise in which a good person may need to sacrifice his or her life and thus foreclose

[35] *Nicomachean Ethics* III.9, 1117b10-16.

any future opportunities for virtuous living. This emerges from the common good being deemed prior, and thus more essential, than the good of any individual. Given the precedence of the state, it should come as no surprise that virtuous individuals may be called upon to sacrifice future personal happiness for the greater good.

In a related vein, Aristotle mentions a self-lover in his discussion on friendship. In defining a self-lover, Aristotle does not mean to imply that such a person loves his own discrete self as would an egoist or narcissist. Instead, Aristotle is referring to the best part of ourselves, which is to say the best part of our soul:

> [A self-lover] assigns to himself the things that are noblest and best, and gratifies the most authoritative element in himself and in all things obeys this; and just as a city or any other systematic whole is most properly identified with the most authoritative element in it, so is a man; and therefore the man who loves this and gratifies it is most of all a lover of self...For the wicked man, what he does clashes with what he ought to do, but what the good man ought to do he does; for the intellect always chooses what is best for itself, and the good man obeys his intellect... In all the actions, therefore, that men are praised for, the good man is seen to assign to himself the greater share in what is noble. In this sense, then, as has been said, a man should be a lover of self; but in the sense in which most men are so, he ought not.[36]

It is his intellect (or understanding) that the good man loves and obeys, because that is the part of himself that most truly defines "self". Consequently, a self-lover is willing to do noble acts even at the cost of his life because what is valued is the virtuous activity of the reasoning part of his soul (which is shared among all normal human beings), and not his composite identity. In doing what is noble

---

[36] *Nicomachean Ethics* IX.8, 1168b29-33, 1169 a12-17 and a34-1169b3.

and loving the best part of his self, the self-lover is one who strives for the common good:

> Those, then, who busy themselves in an exceptional degree with noble actions all men approve and praise; and if all were to strive towards what is noble and strain every nerve to do the noblest deeds, everything would be as it should be for the common good...[37]

The importance Aristotle places on the common good is difficult to overlook or ignore. Doing so risks misunderstanding an essential feature of his philosophy. His concern with the common good is a question I will more fully address in the next chapter, but it should nevertheless be clear that his viewpoint is primarily that of a holist and not of an individualist. As such, he is keen on describing the practical considerations encompassing the realization of the common good in society, and both his ethics and politics can be seen as attempts to address these.

Connected to the importance placed on excellent political activity directed at the common good, Aristotle addresses the rule of states by their best citizens:

> But when a whole family, or some individual, happens to be so pre-eminent in excellence as to surpass all others, then it is just that they should be the royal family and supreme over all, or that this one citizen should be king...For surely it would not be right to kill, or ostracize, or exile such a person, or require that he should take his turn in being governed. The whole is naturally superior to the part, and he who has this pre-eminence is in the relation of a whole to a part. But if so, the only alternative is that he should have the supreme power, and that mankind should

[37] *Nicomachean Ethics* IX.8, 1169a6-10.

> obey him, not in turn, but always.[38]

This same logic of whole to part among citizens within the state can be found in Aristotle's discussion of the relationship of God to the rest of the universe, "For the good is found both in the order and in the leader, and more in the latter; for he does not depend on the order but it depends on him".[39] Virtuous political leaders thus mimic the activity of God by bringing order to the earthly estate, in a manner analogous to the order brought to the universe by God. As mentioned before, that helps explain why Aristotle said that the political life can be happy (if only in a secondary way), despite not being contemplative.

THE HIERARCHY OF ENDS

Despite identifying two kinds of lives that embody happiness (the practical and the contemplative respectively), Aristotle is quite clear that our object should be "complete" happiness:

> Since there are evidently more than one end, and we choose some of these (e.g. wealth, flutes, and in general instruments) for the sake of something else, clearly not all ends are complete ends; but the chief good is evidently something complete. Therefore, if there is only one complete end, this will be what we are seeking. Now we call that which is in itself worthy of pursuit more complete than that which is worthy of pursuit for the sake of something else, and that which is never desirable for the sake of something else more complete than the things that are desirable both in themselves and for the sake of that other thing, and therefore we call complete without qualification

[38] *Politics* III.17, 1288a16-19 and 25-29.

[39] *Metaphysics* XII.10, 1075a13-15.

> that which is always desirable in itself and never for the sake of something else... Now such a thing happiness, above all else, is held to be...[40]

Aristotle here categorizes three kinds of ends: (1) those desirable for the sake of something else, (2) those desirable in themselves and for the sake of something else, and (3) those desirable in themselves and not for the sake of anything else. He then says that *if* there is but one complete end that is desirable in itself and never for the sake of something else, then that is what we are seeking and must be what constitutes happiness.

Beginning in X.6, Aristotle once again picks up the threads of his argument bearing on the complete end for human life, and stating that there is but one complete end and therefore but one measure of happiness:

> And this activity alone [contemplation] would seem to be loved for its own sake; for nothing arises from it apart from the contemplating, while from practical activities we gain more or less apart from the action.[41]

Aristotle thus concludes that practical wisdom is not the chief good because, while it is desirable for itself, it is also desirable for the sake of something else (i.e. the life of contemplation). In addition, Aristotle states that happiness depends upon leisure, but practical activities can be quite un-leisurely and ultimately done for the sake of leisure. As he says, "... we are busy that we may have leisure, and make war

---

[40] *Nicomachean Ethics* I.7, 1097a25-35.

[41] *Nicomachean Ethics* X.7, 1177b1-3.

that we may live in peace".[42] Happiness is therefore defined in terms of contemplation and extends just so far as one contemplates.

As conceived by Kraut, Aristotle's conception of the good human life can be depicted graphically as follows:

A
B
M N
X Y Z

A = theoretical activity
B = ethical activity
M, N = other goods that are desirable in themselves
X, Y, Z = goods that are conditionally desirable.[43]

Complete happiness consists in theoretical activity and represents the target that should guide all other activities. It is that for the sake of which all else is done. Ethical activity, while good in itself, is also done for the sake of theoretical activity. Although it is possible to lead a happy life if one consistently exercises the ethical virtues, it is not the happiest life because it does not partake in divine activity. All the other deeds we undertake, or all the supporting goods we acquire throughout our lives, ought to be done in accordance with the demands of complete happiness.

I think it fair to say that this hierarchical order is an acknowledgment of dependency. Even though contemplation is the chief good, it cannot be fully realized in the absence of subordinate goods. We should strive to lead a philosophical life throughout our lives, but

42 *Nicomachean Ethics* X.7, 1177b5-6.

43 Kraut, 1989, 6.

since we are mortal, and require various other external and bodily goods like food and health, we must satisfy those pre-requisites first. That is why Aristotle repeatedly qualifies his assertion that happiness consists in theoretical virtue. It is the chief good in human life and represents the best kind of life that a human being can lead, but it is simply not possible for any human being to engage in intellectual activity continuously and to the exclusion of our other more basic (but not more important) human needs.

Upon my reading, the basic requirements that are either necessary or contribute to happiness include: (1) virtuous activity, (2) goods of the body, (3) external goods, and (4) a sufficient period of virtuous living. Virtuous activity is happiness itself expressed either with respect to the ethical or theoretical life. By goods of the body, I take Aristotle to be referring to the physical attributes needed for living a virtuous life (e.g. good health). This is important, since happiness is an activity as opposed to some end state or disposition. As such, the sick or disabled would find happiness unattainable insofar as their sickness or disability prohibited them from leading an active life in accordance with either of the intellectual virtues. External goods refer to the things we need found outside of our bodies such as food, clothing, and friends - the lack of which could also inhibit happiness. Finally, it is necessary to engage in virtuous activity for a sufficiently long time (although it is impossible to say just how long) for "one swallow does not a summer make".

What seems clear to me is that Aristotle thought that many of these additional resources could be satisfied only within the context of a political community.[44] As isolated individuals, we simply cannot expect to achieve anything approaching complete happiness. Only within society can people be freed from the tasks of mere survival to engage in the virtuous life - either intellectual or practical. As a consequence, it is only within a good state that citizens can expect to realize their aspirations of living well:

> In the perfect state the good man is absolutely the same as the good citizen; whereas in other states the good citizen is only good relatively to his own form of government.[45]

It is important, therefore, to maintain a good state. It is this fact that explains why a good individual may be required to make sacrifices, perhaps including his or her life, for the greater good. If happiness is the best thing in human life, and it is our function not just to live, but to live well, and our function in turn can be realized only within the context of society, then it stands to reason that the well-being of the state should take priority over that of the individual.

Finally, Aristotle believed that the state was a creation of nature that allows us to fulfill our specific human nature (i.e. our function). Yet it seems evident that we tend to form flawed societies, implying that human beings have great difficulty in being themselves. This is a troubling phenomenon which seems to have induced Aristotle to conclude that happiness may have to be somewhat forced

---

[44] As Aristotle says in *Politics* I.2, 1252b28-30, "When several villages are united in a single complete community, large enough to be nearly or quite self-sufficing, the state comes into existence, originating in the bare needs of life, and continuing in existence for the sake of a good life."

[45] *Politics* IV.7, 1293b5-7.

upon people:

> But it is difficult to get from youth up a right training for excellence if one has not been brought up under right laws; for to live temperately and hardily is not pleasant to most people, especially when they are young. For this reason their nurture and occupations should be fixed by law; for they will not be painful when they have become customary. But it is surely not enough that when they are young they should get the right nurture and attention; since they must, even when they are grown up, practise and be habituated to them, we shall need laws for this as well, and generally speaking to cover the whole of life; for most people obey necessity rather than argument, and punishments rather than what is noble.[46]

Perhaps in this observation can be found a measure of disappointment, given that most people are unable to actualize their function, spending their time instead upon satisfying self-interested desires to the neglect of what is good and noble. This may be the result, at least in part, of the type of government within which we are subjects:

> The first governments were kingships, ...But when many persons equal in merit arose, no longer enduring the pre-eminence of one, they desired to have a commonwealth, and set up a constitution. The ruling class soon deteriorated and enriched themselves out of the public treasury; riches became the path to honour, and so oligarchies naturally grew up. These passed into tyrannies and tyrannies into democracies; for love of gain in the ruling classes was always tending to diminish their number, and so to strengthen the masses, who in the end set upon their masters and established democracies. Since cities have increased in size, no other form of government appears to be any longer even easy to establish.[47]

46 *Nicomachean Ethics* X.9, 1179b31-1180a5.

47 *Politics* III.15, 1286b9, 12-22.

Thus, success of an individual will be at least partly contingent upon the quality of the state or society within which they reside. The difficulty in developing good states limits the capacity to develop good citizens. I would add that an inability to maintain environmental quality is also of importance since it supports the well-being of states. Hence, we can identify important relationships among the quality of the environment, the quality of the state and the quality of a human life.

Aristotle's moral philosophy expresses an ideal; a statement outlining what we as human beings can and ought to achieve based upon our role in the natural world. It is the product of a descriptive biologist who sought to understand the world around him and our place in it. Based upon that understanding we are given a platform from which to survey our position in the natural order. According to Aristotle we have within us the ability to live a life superior to that of the other living things on Earth. As a consequence, when we are at our best, we are the best of all animals. But given the elusiveness of the good life, we can also be the worst of all animals:

> A social instinct is implanted in all men by nature, and yet he who first founded the state was the greatest of benefactors. For man, when perfected, is the best of animals, but, when separated from law and justice, he is the worst of all; ...That is why, if he has not excellence, he is the most unholy and the most savage of animals, and the most full of lust and gluttony.[48]

Humans are curious beings. Despite all of our potential to live a divine like existence and achieve blessedness, we can also fall so very

[48] *Politics* I.2, 1253a30-33, 36-37.

short of the mark and live a life baser and more dissolute than any other creature.

CONCLUSION

The implications of the previous discussion may be disquieting. If it is the case that life can be ordered along a scale from less good to more good, corresponding to how closely it comes to imitating the life of God, then it would appear that the position of human beings along this scale is a contingent variable. Aldo Leopold said that "a thing is right when it tends to preserve the integrity, stability, and beauty of the biotic community. It is wrong when it tends otherwise".[49] Given that Aristotle was also concerned with the collective good (at least with respect to the political community), one wonders if he would agree with Leopold, and what his reaction would be to the political **and** ecological challenges of modern times. Of greater interest, however, is the practical considerations associated with policy planning and implementation based upon a conception of the communal good within a natural hierarchy as applied to modern circumstances. If the good human life can only be achieved within the context of the state, because the state is metaphysically prior to the individual as whole to part, and in the same way the good state is only possible within a good or stable environment, then it stands to reason that the well-being or integrity of the environment has priority over that of the state, which in turn has priority over that of the individual. One can wonder how this calls into question the

[49] Leopold, *A Sand County Almanac: With Essays on Conservation from Round River*, 1966, 262.

preeminence of human interests as compared to the integrity of the biotic community, to use Leopold's phrase. Additionally, since the actual worth (as opposed to potential worth) of human life does not necessarily trump that of other living beings, then it is possible that nonhuman interests could be given greater weight than those of humans in times of conflict. But in order to pursue this matter further, it will be necessary to better articulate the importance placed upon the broader environmental conditions for human life as found in Aristotle's metaphysics.

NOTES

J. L. Ackrill, "Aristotle on Eudaimonia." In *Essays on Aristotle's Ethics*, ed. A. Rorty, (Berkeley: University of California Press, 1980), 15-33.

Richard Kraut, *Aristotle on the Human Good*, (Princeton, NJ: Princeton University Press, 1989).

Aldo Leopold, *A Sand County Almanac: With Other Essays on Conservation from Round River*, (New York: Random House, 1966).

R. G. Mulgan, *Aristotle's Political Theory: An Introduction for Students of Political Theory*, (Oxford: Clarendon Press, 1977).

CHAPTER 3: EXPERIENCING NATURE AND THE DESIRE TO UNDERSTAND

INTRODUCTION

In this chapter, I will endeavor to address some important characteristics of Aristotle's larger philosophical discourse that bear upon my thesis. Of particular significance is the proposal captured by the opening line of the *Metaphysics* stating: "All men by nature desire to know".[1] By this he seems to mean that we as human beings have an innate curiosity and impulse to render the world intelligible. In other words, we have a desire within our beings (helping to constitute our being) that is satisfied by coming to understand not only what the world is and how it works, but also why it is as it is. It is through the active engagement of trying to make sense of the world that, if successful, we come to fulfill the best kind of life that a human being can lead (i.e. the contemplative life).

ART AND NATURE

Aristotle considered the investigation of nature through scientific observation to be of utmost importance. He thought that it was only through encountering the world as experienced by our senses that we can begin to grasp "first principles" and thus come to understand the world and our place in it. As mentioned previously, it was this feature of his philosophical method that distinguished him from the tradition within ancient Greek philosophy that distrusted

1 *Metaphysics* I.1, 980a22.

sense information as a basis for knowledge, and helps explain his natural science contributions. Although he shared the pre-Socratic assumption that the world was relatively easy to understand, he was quick to offer a qualifier:

> The investigation of the truth is in one way hard, in another easy. An indication of this is found in the fact that no one is able to attain the truth adequately, while, on the other hand, no one fails entirely, but every one says something true about the nature of things, and while individually they contribute little or nothing to the truth, by the union of all a considerable amount is amassed. Therefore, since the truth seems to be like the proverbial door, which no one can fail to hit, in this way it is easy, but the fact that we can have a whole truth and not the particular part we aim at shows the difficulty of it.[2]

According to Aristotle, despite truth being like the "proverbial door" which no one can fail to hit, it is not always most evident to us. He concludes that if we cannot understand the world, it is not because the world is an unintelligible place, it is rather because we are beings that tend to be blinded by truth. As he says, "For as the eyes of bats are to the blaze of day, so is the reason in our soul to the things which are by nature most evident of all".[3] In essence, we are beings born into ignorance who must work our way through the mystery nature presents. Once we have made the effort by studying the world around us in all its diversity, we eventually can become aware of the truth. The learning process can be understood as being like walking into bright sunlight from a dark building. Initially, the

2 *Metaphysics* II.1, 993a28-b7.

3 *Metaphysics* II.1, 993b10-11.

surrounding environment is obscured by the greater luminosity of the outdoors. But with time and patience, we have the capacity to see things as they truly are.

In Aristotle's own efforts to render the world intelligible, he came to argue that all living things have a function peculiar to themselves, including human beings. In other words, species can be distinguished from each other by the way they live their lives to realize their own good. The good for the human species was determined to be "... activity of soul in accordance with excellence".[4] Aristotle later concludes that the human good can be more specifically identified with an activity of the rational part of the soul, since it is this part, rather than any of the others, that makes us unique among animals. But in order to fulfill our function, our lives must make the transition from simply living to living well. This entails a transformation from youth to maturity, and in general from ignorance to understanding. Phrased differently, virtue requires that we evolve in a way that is both substantive and directional.

Given that many ancient Greek philosophers looked upon change with a jaundiced eye, it was critical that Aristotle provide an explanation not only of the possibility of change, but its cause (thus securing the legitimacy of sense information). It is with respect to the latter that Aristotle differentiates between things that exist by nature and those by art. For him, natural beings have an inner principle of change:

> All the things mentioned plainly differ from things which are not constituted by nature. For each of them has within itself a principle of motion and of stationariness (in respect of place, or

---

[4] *Nicomachean Ethics* I.7, 1098a17.

> of growth and decrease, or by way of alteration). On the other hand, a bed and a coat and anything else of that sort, qua receiving these designations--i.e. in so far as they are products of art -- have no innate impulse to change.[5]

The cause of change for things that exist by nature is a principle that exists within the thing itself, as opposed to an external force. Organisms, for example, grow and develop as a result of an innate impulse, and not as a result of being molded or crafted as would be the case for a bed.

To give greater clarity to the concept of nature, Aristotle then proceeds in book II of the *Physics* to determine whether nature is to be identified with the matter or form of a natural object. Whereas one account states that the principle of change is to be found in the matter, Aristotle finds this to be an erroneous assumption, since he believes that matter is ultimately dependent upon form. In his account, flesh and bone do not exist as such until form is brought to matter, giving it an order that defines it as flesh and bone. This is a way of saying that matter has the potential to be organized in a particular manner, but the organization itself is brought to it by an additional actually existent principle (i.e. form). It is for this reason that Aristotle says that form is nature rather than matter:

> The form indeed is nature rather than the matter; for a thing is more properly said to be what it is when it exists in actuality than when it exists potentially. Again man is born from man but not bed from bed.[6]

---

5 *Physics* II.1, 192b13-19.

6 *Physics* II.1, 193b7-9.

The form "Human" directs the biological development of an individual human which is a principle internal to all humans. Alternatively, a bed must have the form "bed" imposed upon it externally since beds do not come from other beds. As a consequence, form must be a fully actual additional principle that gives matter the particular order that it has in any specific example. If this actual principle of change or form is internal to the thing itself, then that thing is natural. If the principle of change is external, then it is artificial.

Matter cannot be nature since it is changed without itself causing change. As indicated, Aristotle considers matter to be dependent upon form. It does not exist as such until it receives form and will vary insofar as forms vary.[7] Another important consideration that disqualifies matter as being primary is that it is ultimately unknowable, in the sense that it does not contribute to an understanding of a thing's nature.[8] For example, the form "eye" may be brought to matter resulting in a particular eye. Depending upon the material circumstances involved in making a particular eye, it is possible that one of several different eye colors could result. But the cause of eye color tells us nothing about what it is to be an "eye" insofar as color has nothing to do with the purpose of vision.[9] In a world that is thought to exhibit order and can be rendered intelligible if we make the effort, it stands to reason that matter cannot be fundamental because it does not help understand the "why" or cause of change

7 As he says in *Physics* II.2, 194b8-9, "...matter is a relative thing -- for different forms there is different matter."

8 See *Physics* III.6, 207a25.

9 See *Generation of Animals* V.1, especially 778a18-b19.

in the world. It is form then, that we need to investigate if we want to have knowledge of the world.

Not only did Aristotle consider form to be a cause of change, he also thought it to be the end for the sake of which change occurs:

> ... that for the sake of which, or the end, belongs to the same department of knowledge as the means. But the nature is the end or that for the sake of which. For if a thing undergoes a continuous change toward some end, that last stage is actually that for the sake of which.[10]

I understand him to be saying here that form (since it is nature) is both the end and means to the end. In addition to its being a fully realized state for the sake of which a thing undergoes change, form is also a cause of change directed toward its own realization. For example, a baby raccoon (call him Rocky) grows and develops in order to become a fully functional and mature raccoon. It is the form "Raccoon" that directs the process of Rocky's growth and development for the purpose of completely actualizing "Raccoon" within the particular material circumstances that is Rocky.

Form is thus a force in the world that both causes and directs change. As a cause of change it guides the development of things to a specific end (i.e. fully actualized form). As an end, it provides purpose to the growing organism, for it is that for the sake of which continued development occurs. But in order to be an end, it must be something actual or to have prior existence. Otherwise the process of growth and development would be indeterminate, for how else can something accomplish its potential if that potential remains un-

10 *Physics* II.2, 194a28-31.

defined? As Aristotle says:

> Those who suppose, as the Pythagoreans and Speusippus do, that supreme beauty and goodness are not present in the beginning, because the beginnings both of plants and of animals are causes, but beauty and completeness are in the effects of these, are wrong in their opinion. For the seed comes from other individuals which are prior and complete, and the first thing is not seed but the complete being, e.g. we must say that before the seed there is a man, -- not the man produced from the seed, but another from whom the seed comes.[11]

An immature organism has within it a principle of change that makes the transition from potential to actual form. But to make this transition the actual form "Raccoon" for example, must have been there at the very beginning - not any particular instance of Raccoon such as Rocky, but rather the species-form "Raccoon" of which Rocky is a member.

To appreciate this line of reasoning, I think it important to understand that Aristotle considered living organisms to be not only composites of form and matter,[12] but composites expressing a species-specific form. That is to say there is but one form per species that is shared by all individual members of that species. Even though each organism may differ one from the other, their lives are shaped and directed by the exact same nature. It is for this reason that Aristotle referred to individual animals as a *this* in *this*[13] (i.e. this form

[11] *Metaphysics* XII.7, 1072b32-1073a3.

[12] *Parts of Animals* I.3, 643a24-27.

[13] For example, in *Metaphysics* VII.8, 1034a5-8 Aristotle says, "And when we have the whole, such and such a form in this flesh and in these bones, this is Callias or Socrates; and they are different in virtue of their matter (for that is different), but

in this matter). Therefore, with respect to the growth and development of Rocky, the end his nature is trying to achieve is the same end for all raccoons as such.

THE METHOD OF NATURAL PHILOSOPHY

If we want to understand the "why" of things (i.e. their principles of change and purpose), then it seems we must investigate form. But given that form is purely immaterial, how does Aristotle propose that we initiate our studies? Is there empirical evidence for the presence of form in the world? To this question, I think Aristotle is saying that evidence is clearly available to those who are willing to make the effort to pursue natural philosophy. Therein lies the answer to the former question too, for I believe that Aristotle is signifying that, in investigating the workings of nature and the beings found there, we can ascertain the presence of form. It does not really matter that form (at least as it is found abstracted from its material circumstances) is difficult to appreciate, for evidence can be found throughout nature for its existence:

> Another matter which must not be passed over without consideration is, whether the proper subject of our exposition is that with which the earlier writers concerned themselves, namely, the way each thing is naturally generated, or rather the way it *is*. For there is no small difference between these two views. The best course appears to be that we should follow the method already mentioned -- begin with the phenomena presented by each group of animals, and, when this is done, proceed afterwards to state the causes of those phenomena -- in the case of generation too. For in house building too, these things come about because the form of the house is such and such, rather

---

the same in form; for their form is indivisible."

> than its being the case that the house is such and such because it came about thus.[14]

Aristotle is here saying that we can reason backwards from the phenomena we actually encounter in the world to an understanding of form. This is possible because form is the cause of change and the end for the sake of which change occurs. Consequently, for a being to be such as it is, its form must be "such and such" out of necessity:

> The fittest mode, then, of treatment is to say, a man has such and such parts, because the essence of man is such and such, and because they are necessary conditions of his existence, or, if we cannot quite say this then the next thing to it, namely, that it is either quite impossible for a man to exist without them, or, at any rate, that it is good that they should be there. And this follows: because man is such and such the process of his development is necessarily such as it is; and therefore the part is formed first, that next; and after a like fashion should we explain the generation of all other works of nature.[15]

Curiously, the starting point for natural science must be the end of a thing (i.e. that for the sake of which its development proceeds). Once identified, then it becomes a relatively simple matter of appreciating the significance of each step in the process of development, given that existence is constrained by necessary conditions. As he says, for a being to be "such and such" then its development must be "such as it is".

Although we are studying composites of form and matter, Aristotle makes clear in the same section that the principal object of our

---

14 *Parts of Animals* I.1, 640a12-18.

15 *Parts of Animals* I.1, 640a34-640b4.

research is form:

> But if men and animals and their several parts are natural phenomena, then the natural philosopher must take into consideration flesh, bone, blood, and all the other homogeneous parts; not only these, but also the heterogeneous parts, such as face, hand, foot; and must examine how each of these comes to be what it is, and in virtue of what force. For it is not enough to say what are the stuffs out of which an animal is formed ... For the formal nature is of greater importance than the material nature.[16]

Aristotle is clarifying in this section and others that matter is dependent upon form for its existence. It is form, then, and not matter, that is the primary object of our attention as natural philosophers, even though we must reason backwards from the phenomena presented by material beings to the cause of those phenomena.

With respect to living beings, Aristotle describes soul as being "the form of a natural body having life potentially within it".[17] In this definition, any living being that has an inherent principle of change also has soul (as opposed to artifacts such as beds and houses, which have form imposed upon them externally). To have soul is to have the necessary authority for the maintenance and realization of the living form such as nutrition, perception and reproduction.[18] As such, the soul is the cause of living things:

> The soul is the cause or source of the living body... It is the source of movement, it is the end, it is the essence of the whole living

[16] *Parts of Animals* I.1, 640b18-23, and 28-9.

[17] *On the Soul* II.1, 412a20-21.

[18] *On the Soul* II.

> body ... all natural bodies are organs of the soul. This is true of those that enter into the constitution of plants as well as of those which enter into that of animals. This shows that that for the sake of which they are is soul.[19]

So, it is the case that soul is living form. Although all living things have soul, it is not possible to provide a general definition of soul that can be applied equally well to all species of life.[20] This is because living things exhibit an array of capacities and powers directed toward the actualization of their respective forms. It would therefore be impossible to provide a definition of soul that would give an adequate account of all manifestations of its presence. Plants, for example, have only the power of nutrition, and lack powers common to animals such as sensory experience and locomotion. Of the animals, all have at least one sense (e.g. taste or smell) but may be deficient in others (e.g. sight). In the case of human beings, the additional power of thought and thinking must also be taken into consideration. This is why Aristotle said that an adequate account of soul could be provided only relative to each particular form as it exists in the world as a composite of form and matter.[21]

It is soul, then, that is the divine element in all natural things, and that which brings order to the material property of life. It is also the principal of change and that for the sake of which change occurs in living things. In fulfilling their functions, all individual organisms are seeking to realize their species-specific forms inherited as a poten-

---

19 *On the Soul* II.4, 415b9, 11-12, 18-20.

20 *On the Soul* II.3, 414b25-28.

21 *On the Soul* II.3, 415a12-13.

tiality existing in a composite of form and matter. Via reproduction, all species engage in an activity of soul that allows them to participate in the eternal life of the divine on a rudimentary level (the only avenue open to most animals). Human beings differ in that insofar we engage in virtuous activity of the rational part of soul, we actually have the ability to live the divine life. Our capabilities are such that we can grasp first principles and contemplate the same essences that God does. It would appear that through contemplation, we have the capacity to transcend our particular human material selves to become "Human". And it is this, more than anything else, that separates us from other animals.

SUBSTANCE

Like other Greek philosophers, Aristotle was interested in determining a candidate for substance, that most basic of things upon which everything else depends. Various speculations had previously been offered, ranging from an infinity of atoms to "number".[22] Anaximander, for instance, proposed that substance was not something perceptible through ordinary experience. According to Hargrove, it was this kind of thinking that had the unfortunate effect of encouraging the ancient Greeks to seek knowledge by reason alone, and not by way of sensory experience. Aristotle's conception of substance is not entirely clear, as he appears inconsistent in his treatment of this subject. In the *Categories*, for example, Aristotle indicates that substance should be identified with particulars:

[22] See Hargrove, 1989: 17-18.

> A substance -- that which is called a substance most strictly, primarily, and most of all -- is that which is neither said of a subject nor in a subject, e.g. the individual man or the individual horse.[23]

In this instance, the paradigm of substance is found in the individual man or horse as opposed to the species. But in book VII of the *Metaphysics*, Aristotle seems to be associating substance with form - a much different conception, as illustrated by the parenthetical comment, "By form I mean the essence of each thing and its primary substance".[24] The difference between these two concepts represents the distinction between a species and an individual member of that species. For example, Aristotle's first conception of substance would indicate that a particular like Rocky (our raccoon) is the paradigm. His later conception indicates that "Raccoon", and not Rocky as such, is the appropriate paradigm. So, is it the species-form or the form-bearing particular representative of the species that is our paradigm of substance? According to Lear in *The Desire to Understand*, by the time Aristotle began considering substance in *Metaphysics* VII, he was forced to reexamine his earlier assumptions maintained in the *Categories*. This was due to his having changed his thinking about what qualifies as the primary basis of reality, in light of his conclusion that objects were composites of form and matter. Thus, it was not so much that Aristotle was inconsistent, as that his thinking about substance evolved over time until the only possible candidate left that could satisfy the conditions for substance was spe-

23 *Categories* 5, 2a13-15.

24 *Metaphysics* VII.7, 1032b1-2.

cies-form.[25]

In Book IV of the *Metaphysics*, Aristotle says that there is a science concerned with "being as being".[26] I take this to mean that it is possible to investigate the most basic component of reality, or that which makes it feasible for something "to be". He is concerned here with examining the essential nature of existence, and is therefore trying to take us beyond an investigation of sensible phenomena and into substance itself:

> ...there are many senses in which a thing is said to be, but all refer to one starting-point; some things are said to be because they are substances, others because they are affections of substance, others because they are a process towards substance, or destructions or privations or qualities of substance, or productive or generative of substance, or of things which are relative to substance, or negations of some of these things or of substance itself.[27]

Aristotle is saying that if we want to investigate being as such, then an understanding of substance should be our object, because in all the ways in which something can be said "to be", there will be a relationship to substance. In book VII of the *Metaphysics*, Aristotle says that essence belongs to substance.[28] Essence in turn is what a

---

25 For an explanation of this position I refer you to Lear (1988), specifically chapter 6. Note that his is not the only interpretation of what Aristotle meant by substance. However, I find the argument to be compelling and accept the position that Aristotle's mature philosophy came to equate substance with form.

26 *Metaphysics* IV.1, 1003a22-3.

27 *Metaphysics* IV.2, 1003b5-10.

28 *Metaphysics* VII.4, 1030a28-9.

thing is in virtue of itself.[29] In other words, if you were to strip away all of the accidental qualifications or predications in your description of something, then you would arrive at its essence. For example, musical man is not what a man can be in virtue of himself because being musical is not fundamentally what it is to be a man. To state the essence of some thing is to define what it is at its most basic level, and only substance is definable.[30] Since Aristotle is equating substance with form, then it is the case that when we investigate worldly phenomena and inquire into their causes, we are also examining substance. Worded differently, by studying the forms found in the world as composites of form and matter, we are also inquiring into the ontologically basic structure of reality. It is through this process that we come to render the world intelligible, and make the blaze of truth evident to us.

Toward the end of *Metaphysics* VII, Aristotle complicates things a bit by indicating that there is more than one type of substance:

> We should say what, and what sort of thing, substance is, taking another starting-point; for perhaps from this we shall get a clear view also of that substance which exists apart from sensible substances. Since, then, substance is a principle and a cause, let us attack it from this standpoint.[31]

There would appear to be both sensible substances and those that exist apart from sensible substances. Sensible substances, as I un-

---

29 *Metaphysics* VII.4, 1029b14.

30 *Metaphysics* VII.5, 1031a1.

31 *Metaphysics* VII.17, 1041a7-10.

derstand it, means those that our senses are able to perceive, and that are found materialized in the world. For example, when we see Rocky crossing a road, our perception is of an expression of the form "Raccoon". By substances which exist apart, he means substance that has been abstracted from the material conditions of existence (i.e. form by itself, or form without matter) as an object of thought. He is thus proposing to investigate substance as substance, and therefore being as being in the sense of the essence of a thing, as opposed to some perceptible expression of its essence.

I previously mentioned that Aristotle assumed that the only way to study form, and thus understand the cause of things, was to engage in a systematic inquiry of the composite world of form and matter. The reason for this is that we seldom (if ever) encounter form independent of matter. But form as it exists in association with matter can be found all around us.[32] Therefore, information we collect on form must be achieved in an indirect manner, by reasoning backwards from the end of the developmental process of a composite thing to its principle cause of change. I think what Aristotle is doing by investigating "being as being" is to ratchet things up a notch. We are not limited to studying substance simply as we perceive it in its composite state found in our encounters with the natural world. At some point, we can engage in purely abstract thinking of substance as it exists apart from sensible substances. But before I can address this possibility, it is necessary to gain a greater appreciation of the two substances and their relationship to thinking and perception.

---

[32] See *Parts of Animals* I.5, 644b23-31.

PERCEPTION AND SUBSTANCE

When we sense an object, Aristotle indicates that we quite literally take on the form of that object into the appropriate sense organ. It is as if the form of the object were to make an impression of itself onto our senses:

> Generally, about all perception, we can say that a sense is what has the power of receiving into itself the sensible forms of things without the matter, in the way in which a piece of wax takes on the impress of a signet-ring without the iron or gold; what produces the impression is a signet of bronze or gold, but not *qua* bronze or gold: in a similar way the sense is affected by what is coloured or flavoured or sounding not insofar as each is what it is, but insofar as it is of such and such a sort and according to its form. A primary sense-organ is that in which such a power is seated.[33]

In viewing some composite of form and matter in the world such as a tree, the tree's sensible form makes an impression of itself onto the perceiver's visual sense in the same way "in which a piece of wax takes on the impress of a signet-ring". We do not take on the entire tree itself, matter and all, any more than wax takes on bronze or gold. It is not matter as such that makes the impression on our senses, but rather the sensible form of the object as it exists in its particular material instantiation.[34]

An interesting aspect of this line of reasoning is that Aristotle appears to be saying that the various formal objects in the world

[33] *On the Soul* II.12, 424a18-24.

[34] Keep in mind that by sensible form, I am not referring to the form of a particular tree. Rather, sensible form represents an expression of the form "Tree" that is perceptible. It therefore corresponds to sensible substance as opposed to substance that exists apart from matter.

have a projective force. When we engage in observing things found in the world, it is not metaphorically similar to directing a flash-light on passive objects that merely reflect visual information back to us. Rather, the objects themselves are projecting information (i.e. sensible form) that is received within the appropriate part of the sense faculty. After an object's sensible form is impressed upon our sense(s), we become aware of it in the manner appropriate for each sense (e.g. visually, aurally, tactilely, etc.). Objects of the world then have the capacity *to* **be perceived**, whereas perceivers have the capacity to perceive. But from the standpoint of the perceiver, the change of state that occurs from unawareness to awareness is the result of an external force. In other words, awareness occurs within a perceiver which is brought to it by what is being perceived.[35]

Yet in order to investigate being as being, we need to examine form itself and not merely the expression of form as it affects our senses. To address this problem, Aristotle proceeds to make a comparison between sensible form and form alone, as they relate to sensing and thinking respectively:

> Knowledge and sensation are divided to correspond with the realities, potential knowledge and sensation answering to potentialities, actual knowledge and sensation to actualities. Within the soul the faculties of knowledge and sensation are *potentially* these objects, the one what is knowable, the other what is sensible. They must be either the things themselves or their forms. The former alternative is of course impossible: it is not the

[35] This is not unlike the process of a builder building a house, in that the form "House" is imposed externally by the builder onto his materials. In a similar manner, the sensible form "Raccoon" is impressed onto the appropriate sense faculty of a perceiver.

> stone which is present in the soul but its form.[36]

Aristotle is saying that there are two realities corresponding to knowledge and sensation: potential and actual. An object is potentially sensible or knowable as it exists in the world, even if there is no one actually present to either know or sense the object. In like manner, an intelligent sentient being is potentially knowledgeable and sensible. But when someone actually senses or comes to know an object, then the person is changed from potentially perceptive or knowledgeable to actually perceiving or knowing as the object moves from potentially perceptible and knowable, to being actually perceived and known. The important point, however, is that in the transition from potential to actual knowers or perceivers, the respective faculties themselves actually **become** the form of the thing being perceived or known. As Aristotle says, "...the faculties of knowledge and sensation are *potentially* these [actual] objects". Since it is impossible for our faculties to be the things themselves, given that "it is not the stone which is present in the soul", he concludes that it must be their form.

This equivalence between faculty and the form of an object is brought out more clearly in a section in which Aristotle is discussing the similarity between thinking and sense perception:

> If thinking is like perceiving, it must be either a process in which the soul is acted upon by what is capable of being thought, or a process different from but analogous to that. The thinking part of the soul must therefore be, while impassible, capable of receiving the form of an object; that is, must be potentially identical in

[36] *On the Soul* III.8, 421b24-29.

> character with its object without being the object. Thought must be related to what is thinkable, as sense is to what is sensible.[37]

The thinking part of the soul, like the sensing part, must be capable of receiving the form of an object. Not only that, but it must be identical in character with the object without its being the object. When one senses a raccoon, one's visual faculty does not become that raccoon; it rather becomes the sensible form of "Raccoon" as it exists apart from the matter. But when one knowledgeably thinks about raccoons, the mind becomes form itself (i.e. "Raccoon") as it exists apart from matter. Thus, the sense faculty becomes sensible form or an expression of form "Raccoon,"whereas mind has the potential to become "Raccoon" itself.

In addition, Aristotle emphasizes in this book that it is impossible to understand the world in the absence of sense information, since the objects of both thought and perception are found in sensible things:

> Since it seems that there is nothing outside and separate in existence from sensible spatial magnitudes, the objects of thought are in the sensible forms, viz. both the abstract objects and all the states and affections of sensible things. Hence no one can learn or understand anything in the absence of sense...[38]

In this section, Aristotle is reinforcing the idea that knowledge of things is impossible without an active engagement with the world through our senses. If we want to understand how the world works then we cannot direct our gaze inwards or engage in reason alone.

[37] *On the Soul* III.4, 429a13-18.

[38] *On the Soul* III.8, 432a4-7.

The basis of reality (i.e. substance) is found out in the world and it is only by casting our searching gaze outwards that we can come to understand the structure of reality. In doing so, we are taking on the forms as we encounter them in sensible things. It is because of this capacity as it relates to the thinking part of our soul that we are able to abstract form from the composite world of form and matter and investigate being as being.

THOUGHT AND SUBSTANCE

I mentioned earlier how Aristotle differentiated between sensible and intelligible substances. On my reading, sensible substances represent forms that the senses are capable of perceiving. In fact, the sensible form of an object of perception and the sense faculty capable of perception become one and the same thing. The same relationship holds true for objects of thought, in that the thinking faculty becomes the knowable form as indicated in *On the Soul* III.4, 429a13-18 (quoted above). On this account, we can refer to the object of perception to be sensible form and the object of thought to be intelligible form. An important point is that a thinking being must also be sentient in that knowledge is dependent upon sensory information:

> The senses which operate through external media, viz. smelling, hearing, seeing, are found in all animals which possess the faculty of locomotion. To all that possess them they are a means of preservation in order that, guided by antecedent perception, they may both pursue their food, and shun things that are bad or destructive. But in animals which have also intelligence they serve for the attainment of a higher perfection. They bring in tidings of many distinctive qualities of things, from which knowledge of things both speculative and practical is generated

in the soul.[39]

Thus, a rational being cannot be without a sense faculty, because it is through our senses that we acquire the objects of thought (i.e. form without matter). A person without at least a limited ability to acquire sensory information is in an untenable position from which to acquire knowledge about the world. Aristotle even considered certain senses to have priority over others with respect to their relative contributions to intelligence. He considered seeing to be the superior sense overall, but nevertheless thought that hearing was more significant for thought development. As he says, "Accordingly, of persons destitute from birth of either sense [seeing or hearing], the blind are more intelligent than the deaf and dumb".[40]

Like senses, the various possible faculties are not held in common by all species. All animals have the capacity for perception, but understanding is found in only part.[41] Humans alone appear to be in possession of the rational part of the soul issuing in contemplative activity. It is this ability that provides for the potential (though not necessarily actual) superiority of human life relative to other animals, since this is the activity that occupies God continuously (keeping in mind that the divine life is the absolute standard for happiness). As beings with a rational mind in addition to sentience,

---

39 *Sense and Sensibilia* I.1, 436b18-437a4.

40 *Sense and Sensibilia* I.1, 437a15-16. This indicates to me that Aristotle either was unaware of, or did not accord much significance to nonverbal linguistic systems (i.e. sign language).

41 *On the Soul* III.3, 427b7-9.

we have the ability to take on the intelligible forms of things found in the world. As such, we have the capacity to render the world intelligible given its ultimate intelligibility. This is made possible because by taking on intelligible forms, we are taking on their substance. In fact, the substance of a thing and our minds become one and the same, since thought and the object of thought are identical.

This does not mean that the intelligibility of things comes to us as easily as their perceptibility. As stated at the beginning of this chapter, Aristotle was well aware that what is most evident is not always most evident to us. It takes time to understand the truth of things since the truth is like the "blaze of day to the eyes of bats". To achieve an understanding of things, it is vital that we cast our gaze on the world around us, so that we can become aware of reality through its perception. This mandates that we spend our leisure time in an effort to understand how the world works through active study and participation within it. If, for example, we want to understand what it is to be a raccoon, then we should be willing to actively engage in the study of the various dimensions of raccoon life, from the behavioral and physiological to the ontological. And based upon our sensory experience, we can then begin to abstract forms as they exist as composites of form and matter and get at the "why" of things. In other words, rendering the world intelligible takes both time and effort, but is possible and worthwhile.

Via the process of understanding the world, a knower moves from a bare potential to know to actually knowing.[42] In other words,

[42] *On the Soul* II.5, 417a21-30 makes this distinction.

a person can be a knower in two senses: potentially and actually. A potential knower is one with the capacity to understand, but this capacity remains undeveloped. All normal human beings are knowers in this sense. An actual knower is one who has successfully made the necessary effort to understand things. He or she has moved from beyond the bare capacity to understand, to an actual understanding. Human beings are therefore capable of exhibiting a range of facultative capacities, from bare potential to fully actual. The primary difference between a knower and a perceiver is that an actual knower can contemplate an object of thought whenever he or she wants without the object being physically present:

> Actual sensation corresponds to the stage of the exercise of knowledge. But between the two cases compared there is a difference; the objects that excite the sensory powers to activity, the seen, the heard, etc., are outside. The ground of this difference is that what actual sensation apprehends is individuals, while what knowledge apprehends is universals, and these are in a sense within the soul itself. That is why a man can think when he wants to but his sensation does not depend upon himself -- a sensible object must be there.[43]

Aristotle is here saying that our sense faculty takes on the sensible form as found in particular instances. Although the form is the same in all species of object, it is manifested in as many ways as there are individual instances of that form in matter. When we perceive Rocky for example, our perception is of an expression of "Raccoon" as found in the composite that is Rocky. This means we can never take on the sensible form "Raccoon" in abstraction of the material

[43] *On the Soul* II.5, 417b19-27.

and individual circumstances of its existence because sensible form is a force in the world acting on a sense faculty that is passive. On the other hand, as an object of active thought "Raccoon" has been fully abstracted from the material world and has become a part of the soul. Once we understand what it is to be a raccoon, our soul takes on an order corresponding to the order of reality (i.e. we have mastered the subject matter). The intelligible form has been indelibly etched on our souls, so to speak, and if we choose to contemplate the essence of "Raccoon-ness", we can do so at any time without external stimulation because the knowledge of "Raccoon" has been internalized.

But we can also look at things from the perspective of the object of thought or of perception. As mentioned previously, the sensible forms of objects represent a force in the world. It is by virtue of their own projective power that suitably placed perceivers are able to become aware of an object. Narrowly speaking, perceivers amount to nothing more than passive receivers of sensible form that is brought to them from the outside. The sensible form of an object is imposed upon the sense faculty in the same way that the form of a house is brought to bricks and mortar. It is the case then that the sensible form of a thing also exists as potentiality and actuality. It has the potential of being perceived and if the conditions are right (a perceiver perceiving) it will actually be perceived. The same holds true of intelligible form in that it can be both potentially and actually understood. Given that perception and thought are one and the same with the objects of each (i.e. actualized form), then from the perspective of the object, we can speak of its being a fundamental force in the world that can become either perceived or understood. With respect to the later possibility, Lear says:

> All embodied forms are thus potentialities for their own self-understanding. Aristotelian essences, one might say, are a force for their own self-understanding. The achieved self-understanding is the form itself in a disembodied state.[44]

Human beings can understand the world by taking on the intelligible forms of things (via perception) as objects of thought. From the standpoint of the human, the world becomes intelligible and the human soul takes on a certain order corresponding to the order of reality (i.e. we acquire knowledge). If it is true, as Aristotle says, that humans have a desire to understand, then once human mind becomes substance through rigorous study of form as found in the world, that desire has been satisfied. But from the perspective of embodied forms, human understanding can be seen as the actualization of a desire to be understood, since the embodied form and the object of thought are identical. Thus, when human mind takes on form it becomes that form. In trying to understand raccoon life, for example, the human mind becomes "Raccoon". For all intents and purposes, understanding of "Raccoon" for the human is the selfsame activity as self-understanding for "Raccoon".

Humans are unique among animals in that when we understand what it is to be human, we actualize the potential for self-understanding within our own souls. Other perishable beings lack the capacity for self-understanding within their own souls, because they

---

[44] Lear, 1988: 131.

lack a rational part of soul, and thus cannot take on intelligible form. For other natural beings, self-understanding can take place only externally in the mind of an individual actively rendering form intelligible. Thus, they are dependent upon a being capable of contemplating the essence of being to fully actualize their specific form.[45]

GOD

I think we can look at Aristotle's world as consisting of two parts, each of which is concerned with the realization of form. The first part is the natural world of everyday experience, in which we encounter form as embodied in composites of form and matter. In this component, life can be understood as an ongoing process caused by an internal principle of change aimed at the realization of species-form. The second part is the world of form alone or as substance as it exists apart from sensible substances, and aimed at the realization of intelligible form. In both parts, we can find form as it exists along a continuum from potentiality to actuality, keeping in mind that the goal of both parts is the realization of form to the fullest extent (i.e.

[45] I do not mean to imply that part of what it is to be a representative member of a species is that it be understood or that it achieves self-understanding, or that it is in some way dependent upon human beings for its development. Rather, I am interpreting Aristotle as saying that each species-form has the capacity to be understood and that with respect to human beings, our ability to understand any species-form is dependent upon its manifesting a projective force in the world that can result in perception and makes possible our contemplation of that species-form. An interesting by-product of our contemplating a given species-form is that what is understanding for us is self-understanding for the form being contemplated, since thought and the object of thought are the same. Self-understanding is thus a part of human nature, not of non-human nature (exclusive of God), although the end result (i.e. understanding) is the same for both the form being contemplated and the individual human being who satisfies his or her specific desire to understand the world.

to become actual):

> ...things that are posterior in becoming are prior in form and in substance, e.g. man is prior to boy and human being to seed; for the one already has its form, and the other has not. Secondly, because everything that comes to be moves towards a principle, i.e. an end. For that for the sake of which a thing is, is its principle, and the becoming is for the sake of the end; and the actuality is the end, and it is for the sake of this that the potentiality is acquired.[46]

It is important to keep in mind that by actuality, Aristotle is referring to an activity and not primarily to something apart from action:

> ...the action is the end, and the actuality is the action. Therefore even the word 'actuality' is derived from 'action', and points to fulfillment. And while in some cases the exercise is the ultimate thing (e.g. in sight the ultimate thing is seeing, and no other product besides this results from sight), but from some things a product follows (e.g. from the art of building there results a house as well as the act of building), yet none the less the act is in the former case the end and in the latter more of an end than the mere potentiality is.[47]

Even in those activities that result in a product, such as building a house, the actuality and thus the end is to be found more in the activity leading to the product than in the product itself. With respect to natural beings with an internal principle of change, the actuality is a "living". Therefore, the proper end of natural beings is the realization of form as manifested as a way of living.

In this bipartite order, I think we can better grasp the possibility

---

[46] *Metaphysics* IX.8, 1050a4-10.

[47] *Metaphysics* IX.8, 1050a22-28.

of two kinds of lives that can be said to be happy in Aristotle's *Nicomachean Ethics*, for human beings are able to participate in both parts of existence. As animals, we live perishable lives as composites of form and matter. As thinkers, we live the metaphysical life of form alone. It is in the former life that we can become happy to a secondary degree, because if we organize our lives according to the ethical virtues, then we are in a good position to realize fully and sustain human form as it exists as a composite of form and matter. In the latter, we can live a life that is best, because it is through contemplation that the fullest actualization of form is achieved, beyond what is possible in the composite world.[48] Since contemplation is the fullest actualization of form as such (i.e. not just of human form), when human beings contemplate the essences found in the world, we are simply living the best life as such, and not just the best *human* life. Although the *Nicomachean Ethics* addresses the question of "what is the good life for human beings?", Aristotle is really providing an answer that would be applicable to any natural being capable of rational thought.

But all of this is impossible unless there is a prior actuality for the sake of which the potentiality is acquired. In Aristotle's world, every potentiality must be preceded by an actuality.[49] It is from this

48 This is because contemplation is the only actuality that is an end in itself. As Aristotle says in the *Nicomachean Ethics* X.7-8, "If happiness is activity in accordance with excellence, it is reasonable that it should be in accordance with the highest excellence...And this activity alone would seem to be loved for its own sake; for nothing arises from it apart from the contemplating, while from practical activities we gain more or less apart from the action."

49 This can be expressed in terms that do not violate the principle of non-contradiction. Basically, this argues that whatever exists cannot not be. Therefore, even

perspective that Aristotle comes to regard as necessary an eternal unmovable substance that acts as the prior actuality of all existing things. Otherwise, if all substances were perishable, then all things would be perishable (which would be untenable):

> For substances are the first of existing things, and if they are all destructible, all things are destructible. But it is impossible that movement should either come into being or cease to be; for it must always have existed.[50]

In providing a basis for an eternal substance, Aristotle is establishing the ontological independence of primary substance, or that substance upon which all reality ultimately depends. As such, it represents the highest end or that for the sake of which all things exist. It is thus analogous to the chief good that Aristotle speaks of in the *Nicomachean Ethics*, in the sense that the contemplative life is the end for the sake of which we ought to organize the entire structure of our lives.

An eternal unmovable substance is God by another name. All motion and change in the world can be considered a response to God, for God is the final cause of movement and thus of change. In fact, Lear[51] interprets Aristotle as saying that the order of the world as a whole is an attempt to realize physically the order of God's

---

if something exists as a mere potentiality it must nevertheless actually exist. As Aristotle says in *Metaphysics* IX.8, 1050b17: "Nothing, then, which is without qualification imperishable is without qualification potentially; ...imperishable things, then, exist actually."

[50] *Metaphysics* XII.6, 1071b5-8.

[51] Lear, 1988: 296.

thought. By thinking the substances that make up the world, God is establishing their actuality and providing both the cause of change in the world and the end for the sake of which change occurs. Like moths to a flame, all things are drawn to the full realization of form made actual by divine contemplation. In addition, by thinking substances as a whole, God is establishing the actuality of the world as a whole. It is the divine activity of contemplation that Aristotle considers to be the best activity in the fullest sense:

> On such a principle [God], then, depend the heavens and the world of nature. And its life is such as the best which we enjoy, and enjoy for but a short time ... And thought in itself deals with that which is best in itself, and that which is thought in the fullest sense with that which is best in the fullest sense.[52]

By our thinking substances, we also participate in an activity that is best in the absolute. In addition, by thinking substances our mind becomes that substance at its highest level of actuality. But given that we are not God, we cannot enjoy the best kind of life indefinitely.

One of the more intriguing characteristics of Aristotle's philosophy is his conception of the order of reality as being an expression of desire for God:

> There is, then, something which is always moved with an unceasing motion, which is motion in a circle; and this is plain not in theory only but in fact. Therefore the first heavens must be eternal. There is therefore also something which moves them. And since that which is moved and moves is intermediate, there is a mover which moves without being moved, being eternal, substance, and actuality. And the object of desire and the object of thought move in this way; they move without being moved.

52 *Metaphysics* XII.7, 1072b14-15, 18-20.

The primary objects of desire and of thought are the same.[53]

The primary object of thought is actual substance - the principle of change and that for the sake of which a thing exists. Since God thinking substance is substance at its highest level of actuality, and since the object of thought and of desire are the same, then the striving to realize form to the fullest is also an expression of desire for God. This desire is expressed by all life, for God thinks all substances. In striving to realize their form, every living thing is trying to partake of divine activity. If the plants and animals of the perishable world fail to achieve their goal, it will not be due to lack of effort. They participate in divine activity in as far as they are able, given that they are not endowed with a capacity for taking on intelligible form. What all living things have in common, however, is a nutritive and reproductive power of soul that sustains them both as individuals and as species. It is through these two activities that all living things participate in the eternal and divine:

> It follows that first of all we must treat of nutrition and reproduction, for the nutritive soul is found along with all the others and is the most primitive and widely distributed power of soul, being indeed that one in virtue of which all are said to have life. The acts in which it manifests itself are reproduction and the use of food, because for any living thing that has reached its normal development and which is unmutilated, and whose mode of generation is not spontaneous, the most natural act is the production of another like itself, an animal producing an animal, a plant a plant, in order that, as far as its nature allows, it may partake in the eternal and divine. That is the goal towards which all things strive, that for the sake of which they do whatsoever

[53] *Metaphysics* XII.7, 1072a21-27.

their nature renders possible.[54]

Individual beings must have food in order to survive. But being mortal, even those who have met their nutritional needs and have been spared misfortune cannot live forever. The only avenue left is to sustain the species-form whose actuality is both the cause and purpose of the individual's existence. By way of reproduction, individual beings maintain their essence through time, and thus come as close to immortality as their nature allows, not as the self-same individual but rather the same form:

> Since then no living thing is able to partake in what is eternal and divine by uninterrupted continuance (for nothing perishable can for ever remain one and the same), it tries to achieve that end in the only way possible to it, and success is possible in varying degrees; so it remains not indeed as the self-same individual but continues its existence in something like itself -- not numerically but specifically one.[55]

Aristotle is here indicating that what is being preserved is species-form, which is the same for all individuals of a species. Recall that all individual species were characterized by Aristotle as being *this* form in *this* matter. As such, individual organisms within a species share the same nature making them "specifically one".

Not only is God the cause of all species, but of the world's order taken as a systematic whole. God brings structure to the cosmos as a whole, because God's thinking is indivisible:

---

54 *On the Soul* II.4, 415a23-b1.

55 *On the Soul* II.4, 415b3-8.

> It is clear then from what has been said that there is a substance which is eternal and unmovable and separate from sensible things. It has been shown also that this substance cannot have any magnitude, but is without parts and indivisible.[56]

According to Aristotle, everything that is without matter is indivisible. Since God is eternal substance, his thinking cannot be like a multiplexer moving from one component of existence to the next. Rather, it must be a thinking of the whole, and it is the cosmic response to his holistic thinking that brings the order to the universe that Aristotle thought empirically evident. It is this indivisible nature of God's thinking that makes the world a good place:

> We must consider also in which of two ways the nature of the universe contains the good or the highest good, whether as something separate and by itself, or as the order of the parts. Probably in both ways, as an army does. For the good is found both in the order and in the leader, and more in the latter; for he does not depend on the order but it depends on him.[57]

The highest good is God himself, for it is he who gives order to the universe. But the cosmos too is good, although it is difficult to make the separation between them. For it would appear on this conception that the cosmos *is* God, in the same way that life *is* God.[58] It then follows that the world is a good place, and the various living things that reside in the world have a share of goodness. This is not to say, however, that Aristotle considered absolutely everything in the

---

[56] *Metaphysics* XII.7, 1073a4-6.

[57] *Metaphysics* XII.10, 1075a11-15.

[58] See *Metaphysics* XII.7, 1072b26-31.

world to be good. Clearly this is not the case, especially as it relates to the lives of human beings, given our tendency to act contrary to our nature. But there is a fundamental goodness to be found in the world, both as a whole and as parts constituting the whole, insofar as it is made possible by God, and reflects a desire for the highest good that is God.

CONCLUSION

In Aristotle's world, human beings are unique among species in that we are able to bridge the gap between the composite world of form and matter and the world of form alone. We are also the only living beings capable of fully realizing our potential within our own beings. In other words, we alone among the many species of life on Earth are independently capable of self-understanding. This comes as a consequence of the effort to satisfy our desire to know why the world is as it is. As we work our way through what puzzles us about the world in an attempt to make what is most evident most evident to us, the realization dawns that the world is constituted by understanding. It is the actuality toward which all things strive (including human beings), bringing definition to "being".

As best I can determine, Aristotle, in his own efforts to satisfy his desire to understand the world around him, has attempted to develop a metaphysical and ethical system that forms a coherent whole. At the base of reality is God. whose continuous activity of contemplation gives actuality to the world. The rest of the world as manifested in its order and particularity is an attempted realization of God's own self-understanding. By living the contemplative life, human beings are fulfilling their form to its fullest by satisfying the desire to know. A life devoted to contemplation is the best life for a human being to lead, because it is the end towards which human nature is drawn. It is the most blessed of human lives because it incorporates the most blessed of activities.

What I find particularly fascinating about Aristotle's philosophy is that it is thoroughly embedded in the physical world. The human good cannot be realized in abstraction of the world of everyday sensory experience. Happiness is in fact utterly dependent upon encounters with the world to be possible. This is as true for secondary happiness as it is for perfect happiness, since both lives are constituted by activities constrained by the physical world as part to whole. This is especially true for the contemplative life, since only by investigating nature can we understand the forms found in the world. The consequence of this is that the richness of human life is directly related to the richness of life expressing the richness of God.

NOTES

Eugene C. Hargrove, *Foundations of Environmental Ethics*, (Englewood Cliffs: Prentice-Hall, 1989).

Jonathan Lear, *Aristotle: The Desire to Understand*, (New York: Cambridge University Press, 1988).

CHAPTER 4: HUMAN LIFE IN CONTEXT

INTRODUCTION

According to Aristotle, desire pervades the living world and provides an explanation for its growth and development. To have a nature (or be a natural entity), is to have an inner principle of change, motivated by desire, aimed at the appropriate end or *telos* of a given natural being. For any species of life, the proper end is the realization of their species-specific form, and its perpetuation through reproduction defined within ecological dependency. Human beings are unique among animals in that our nature does not come about naturally or without assistance. We thus may fail to realize our nature by desiring things we ought not, or desiring things we ought, but for the wrong reasons. Success in realizing our nature and in becoming happy or blessed is thus contingent upon developing the appropriate virtues within society that allows us to organize our desires and activities, in the absence of misfortune, in a way that fosters the emergence of our true nature, and allows us to be successful in life.

The first step involves developing a firm character built upon ethical virtue. This is to say that an individual must not only choose the ethical life but also do so for the right reasons based upon the inherent value of the virtues themselves. Once individuals have attained practical wisdom, they are then able to seek the intellectual life and the attainment of philosophical wisdom – the best kind of life available to men. In this chapter I want to emphasize that success in living well is made possible in no small measure by the support provided by the state – in particular by providing needed resources (e.g. education, social stability, economic opportunity, etc.) to not only survive, but prosper. By extension, the viability of political institutions is dependent upon environmental stability, since the state is a part of nature. Further, success in attaining philosophical wisdom is dependent upon environmental stability not only with respect to obtaining the practical goods needed for living, but also for supplying form as an object of contemplation needed for living well. An important conclusion in this chapter is that a biologically diverse world offers the opportunity to experience a richer ethical and intellectual life.

THE ORGANIZATION OF DESIRE

As discussed in the previous chapter on metaphysics, it was Aristotle's idea that all life expresses a desire for God. Soul-bearing beings strive to realize their form made actual and intelligible by the eternal contemplative activity of the unmoved mover. This desire is fulfilled within humans most fully via the contemplative life, but can also find expression via practical deliberation. For other animals, desire is coupled with "imagination" to provide the motive force and means for realizing their good:

> To sum up, then, and repeat what I have said, inasmuch as an animal is capable of desire it is capable of self-movement; it is not capable of desire without possessing imagination; and all imagination is either calculative or sensitive. In the latter all animals partake.[1]

---

1 *On the Soul* III.10, 433b27-30. In the revised Oxford translation, "appetite" is used instead of "desire." I am here accepting the translation of Lear (1988) as being more accurate. For clarification see Lear (1988), page 142.

Aristotle refers to imagination as a kind of thinking that can determine the means needed to satisfy a given desire.[2] For example, a carnivore will exercise his sensitive imagination through hunting behavior in order to alleviate hunger.

The calculative imagination contrasts with the sensitive in that the former is produced by the rational part of the soul. Calculation thus embodies a process aimed at the satisfaction of higher order desires, or those concerned with something beyond basic appetites, such as for food and reproduction. Calculation in turn may involve either practical or speculative thinking. Practical thinking deliberates about the variable and contingent aspects of living well within society. Speculative thinking seeks to contemplate first principles, or invariable things such as scientific truth. An important difference between deliberation and contemplation is that the former activity is concerned with reaching an end subject to rational reflection, whereas the latter is an end in itself (i.e. deliberation initiates movement towards an end whereas contemplation is an object of desire itself). They further differ according to the character of the end being addressed - the ethical and intellectual life respectively.

In his discussion of desire, Aristotle provides us with an explanation of change as self-movement. Natural beings have within them an inner principle of change directed toward the realization of form. In fact, and as mentioned in the previous chapter, form is both the end and the cause of change. Desire, as an essential component of living form, motivates natural beings to realize their potential,

---

2 See *On the Soul* III.10, 433a9-21.

and thus stimulates movement toward that goal. Deliberation then represents an activity designed to make movement possible by determining the appropriate means, relative to the desired goal. Metaphorically, deliberation could be equated with bridge building in that our goal is similar to overcoming a barrier to movement. Reaching the other side is not possible until a means (i.e. a bridge) has been erected. Aristotle describes deliberation as a process of reasoning backwards from the desired goal:

> We deliberate not about ends but about what contributes to ends. For a doctor does not deliberate whether he shall heal, nor an orator whether he shall convince, nor a statesman whether he shall produce law and order, nor does any one else deliberate about his end. Having set the end they consider how and by what means it is to be attained; and if it seems to be produced by several means they consider by which it is most easily and best produced, while if it is achieved by one only they consider how it will be achieved by this and by what means this will be achieved, till they come to the first cause, which in the order of discovery is last.[3]

We do this, he says, because we deliberate about the realization of ends and not the ends themselves. Deliberation is thus a form of imagination. Recall that this is the same method Aristotle used in his biological studies to ascertain what it is to be a particular kind of animal striving to actualize its form. For example, to determine what it is to be a raccoon, it is first necessary to discover the end of the species "Raccoon". Based upon this information, we can begin to understand why a particular raccoon like Rocky grew and developed in the observed manner, given that raccoon ontogeny is

3 *Nicomachean Ethics* III.3, 1112b12-19.

driven by necessity.

So, it is the case that desire is an important force within beings having soul. To satisfy desire, all living things exercise their imagination at whatever level available to them in order to secure the requisite means. For human beings, the imaginative capacity is more sophisticated (if not more complicated) in that we possess a rational part of soul capable of either deliberation or contemplation. Because of the increased complexity of human life, it is critically important to organize one's desires for the purpose of living a good human life. Otherwise, we may be tempted to desire things we ought not, or not to desire things we ought. That we are fallible beings and can be mistaken about what constitutes the good life was of concern to Aristotle. By presenting us with his thinking reflected in the *Nicomachean Ethics* and the *Politics,* I believe he attempts to provide a guide to fulfilling our nature by organizing our desires in such a way that we desire nothing amiss.

PRACTICAL WISDOM

For Aristotle, the good life for human beings is one that fulfills human nature as an object of desire. As mentioned previously, Aristotle distinguishes between the good life and the best life achievable. A good life is one that is lived in accordance with ethical virtue, whereas the best life is one lived in accordance with intellectual virtue. What is held in common by both lives is their expression in harmony with the relevant excellence. It is not enough to simply live a certain kind of life that makes it good, it must be lived for the right reason, to the right extent, and in the right way. It is for this reason that Aristotle describes virtue as a state of character that makes a person and the life he leads good:

> We may remark, then, that every excellence both brings into good condition the thing of which it is the excellence and makes the work of that thing be done well; e.g. the excellence of the eye makes both the eye and its work good; for it is by the excellence of the eye that we see well. Similarly the excellence of the horse makes a horse both good in itself and good at running and at carrying its rider and at awaiting the attack of the enemy. Therefore, if this is true in every case, the excellence of man also will be the state which makes a man good and which makes him do his own work well.[4]

A good person has a definite character capable of navigating his way along the path of good living by organizing his desires in the proper way and for the right reasons. When a good person chooses to act justly or temperately for example, he does so because of the inherent value of justice and temperance, and not for reasons of utility.

Being of good character satisfies one of the three prerequisites Aristotle identifies as being necessary for virtuousness.[5] The first is to have knowledge of the virtues. This enables a person to recognize when and under what circumstances virtuous behavior is required. With respect to the giving and taking of money, for example, a person of good character would be of a liberal or magnificent nature, giving and taking neither too much nor too little relative to his means.[6] The second condition is that the agent must choose

4 *Nicomachean Ethics* II.6, 1106a15-23.

5 *Nicomachean Ethics* II.4, 1105a30-b1.

6 *Nicomachean Ethics* II.7, 1107b9-21.

virtuous acts, and choose them for their own sake. In being liberal with regard to money, a person acts in this way because it is the right thing to do under the circumstances. He does not choose to be liberal for reasons inconsistent with the inherent value of liberality itself. The third condition is that the action must proceed from a firm character. Liberality in a man of good character does not occur by accident or under duress - he knows that it is the right thing to do and acts liberally for that reason:

> Actions, then, are called just and temperate when they are such as the just or the temperate man would do; but it is not the man who does these that is just and temperate, but the man who also does them *as* just and temperate men do them. It is well said, then, that it is by doing just acts that the just man is produced, and by doing temperate acts the temperate man; without doing these no one would have even a prospect of becoming good.[7]

The idea that people should choose virtuous acts for their own sake brings up an important distinction that Aristotle discusses early on in the *Nicomachean Ethics* between ends distinct from actions and actions that are ends:

> Every art and every inquiry, and similarly every action and choice, is thought to aim at some good; and for this reason the good has rightly been declared to be that at which all things aim. But a certain difference is found among ends; some are activities, others are products apart from the activities that produce them. Where there are ends apart from the actions, it is the nature of the products to be better than the activities.[8]

---

7 *Nicomachean Ethics* II.4, 1105b5-11.

8 *Nicomachean Ethics* I.1, 1094a1-5.

Not only are there many ends among the things we do, but there are also many things we do that are ends. In modern terminology, we would say that certain activities or products of activities are inherently valuable. For example, a virtuous human being is good in himself, as are his virtuous acts (keeping in mind that the good person is good only to the extent that he lives according to the virtues). The important point to retain in mind, however, is that human well-being is constituted by virtuous activity. In other words, happiness **is** virtuous activity. In a way, we could say that happiness is the product of virtuous activity, but the product in this case *is the activity itself*, the two being one and the same.

Following Kraut, I have argued that happiness consists in two types of virtuous activity that are qualitatively distinct. Complete happiness is made possible by engaging in virtuous intellectual activity. A happy person in this instance will strive to spend as much time as possible in the contemplation of first principles. A qualitatively lower level of happiness is made feasible by engaging in virtuous ethical activity. The former person is said to have philosophical wisdom whereas the latter person has practical wisdom. Being of good character, each person chooses to act virtuously for its own sake. The difference between the two activities is that the first (i.e. contemplation) is done for its own sake and not for the sake of anything further, whereas the second (i.e. practical deliberation) is done both for its own sake **and** for the sake of contemplation.

It was evident to Aristotle that in choosing to act virtuously, one must do so with the right end in mind. As a result, a practically wise person is able not only to deliberate well regarding how to secure the means to an end, but also to ascertain correctly the end upon which to deliberate:

> But excellence in deliberation is a certain correctness of deliberation; hence we must first inquire what deliberation is and what it is about. And, there being more than one kind of correctness, plainly excellence in deliberation is not any and every kind; for the incontinent man and the bad man will reach as a result of his calculation what he sets himself to do, so that he will have deliberated correctly, but he will have got for himself a great evil. Now to have deliberated well is thought to be a good thing; for it is this kind of correctness of deliberation that is excellence in deliberation, viz. that which tends to attain what is good.[9]

Not just any end should be the subject of deliberation. A bad man may display excellence in deliberation, but with an evil end in mind. However well-constructed, charting a path to a bad end does not display the proper excellence in deliberation. Contrary to what Aristotle said previously, it appears that he is now saying that we can deliberate about means and ends in that we must choose the correct end, in order to engage in excellence of deliberation. As such, Aristotle makes practical wisdom dependent upon identifying the proper goal for deliberation. This clearly suggests that the person having philosophical wisdom must of necessity have practical wisdom as well. Otherwise the potential contemplator would be without the means to choose the right target to satisfy the desire to know. If we deliberate correctly about means and ends, then we are in a position to organize our desires into a harmonious whole, giving purposeful structure to our lives. Of course, deliberation is of little consequence if we fail to identify the proper end to be sought. Stat-

9 *Nicomachean Ethics* VI.10, 1142b16-22.

ed more positively, to fulfill our unique potential, it will be critical to pinpoint the right objective providing the proper direction to life. As Aristotle says, "Will not the knowledge of it, then, have a great influence on life? Shall we not, like archers who have a mark to aim at, be more likely to hit upon what we should?".[10] The ability to fulfill our nature as a social animal with human soul hinges upon our ability to identify our proper end. Choosing the wrong end is a prescription for meaninglessness, if not evil, in the world, because it does not address our specific function, and sets us on a path contrary to our nature.

That we could live in a manner at odds with our nature may seem oddly "unnatural". This is especially true when we consider that Aristotle assumes other animals regularly fulfill their own particular natures. In fact, the basis for coming to understand the essence of other animals is contingent upon the empirical analysis of the end for the sake of which they grow and develop. If animals did not regularly fulfill their natural functions, then there would be no basis for understanding animal life on earth, and thus of rendering the world intelligible. Aristotle reconciles this apparent conflict by claiming that virtue is not something that arises in human beings by nature. Even though human beings have a nature, and happiness consists in fully realizing that nature, happiness itself does not come about spontaneously or without effort. As a consequence, human nature effectively becomes both an empirical and a normative concept. It is for this reason that Aristotle takes pains to emphasize the

---

10 *Nicomachean Ethics* I.2, 1094a22-25.

importance of instilling virtuous behavior through habituation:

> ...moral excellence comes about as a result of habit, when also its name is one that is formed by a slight variation from the word for 'habit'. From this it is also plain that none of the moral excellences arises in us by nature; for nothing that exists by nature can form a habit contrary to its nature. For instance the stone which by nature moves downwards cannot be habituated to move upwards, not even if one tries to train it by throwing it up ten thousand times; nor can fire be habituated to move downwards, nor can anything else that by nature behaves in one way be trained to behave in another. Neither by nature, then, nor contrary to nature do excellences arise in us; rather we are adapted by nature to receive them, and are made perfect by habit.[11]

Aristotle reasons that since most men form habits contrary to their own nature, then moral excellence must not be something that arises in us by nature. We must be habituated to engage in virtuous activity in order to adopt an excellent way of life. Fortunately, we have a natural proclivity to receive and accept the virtues despite lacking natural virtue. It is as if we are born with our characters unassembled - all the right materials are there, but in no particular order. For people to become virtuous, then, it seems some assembly is required.

To a large extent, the task of instilling the virtues in people is delegated to the state:

> ...for legislators make the citizens good by forming habits in them, and this is the wish of every legislator; and those who do not effect it miss their mark, and it is in this that a good

---

[11] *Nicomachean Ethics* II.1, 1103a16-25.

> constitution differs from a bad one.[12]

This is also what makes politics the master art, since its proper role is the establishment of a good society, built with good citizens, and for the purpose of propagating good citizens. Since socially isolated individuals cannot be expected to instill habits within themselves, then human beings must associate with others in order to become happy. I think this, as much as anything, expresses why Aristotle thought that human beings are a political species. Happiness is beyond our reach unless structure is brought to our lives within society by "assembling" our characters in such a way that we come to adopt virtuous behavior as our own through good habits. And this is critically important:

> Thus, in one word, states arise out of like activities. This is why the activities we exhibit must be of a certain kind; it is because the states correspond to the differences between these. It makes no small difference, then, whether we form habits of one kind or of another from our very youth; it makes a very great difference, or rather *all* the difference.[13]

Once we have organized our desires with the help of others, then the virtuous habits that originally were painful are transformed into pleasurable activities:

> For moral excellence is concerned with pleasures and pains; it is on account of pleasure that we do bad things, and on account of pain that we abstain from noble ones. Hence we ought to have been brought up in a particular way from our very youth, as Pla-

12 *Nicomachean Ethics* II.1, 1103b3-6.

13 *Nicomachean Ethics* II.1, 1103b20-26.

> to says, so as both to delight in and to be pained by the things that we ought; for this is the right education.[14]

The person who has organized her desires so that they are aimed at the right target, for the right reasons, and in the right way, takes pleasure in the life she leads. Pleasure does not come as an adventitious charm to the ethical person, but is inherent to ethical activity itself. In a way, the process of moral education is concerned with converting pain into pleasure and pleasure into pain. Learning to become happy is not easy, and can be filled with discomfort, yet the person who perseveres with the necessary support will come to realize the importance of her ethical education, and will eventually take pleasure in the ethical life as a partial fulfilment of her own true nature.

PHILOSOPHICAL WISDOM

Happiness depends upon practical wisdom, or a life that is guided according to the ethical virtues. But the ethical life, in and of itself, is not the best life that a human being can lead. To achieve complete happiness, we should engage in intellectual activity as embodied in the life of contemplation, for it is only through this type of activity of the soul that we fully actualize our nature. Philosophical activity is therefore the chief good, or the ultimate end that we are seeking, and is that for the sake of which we lead an ethical life. Although living the life in accordance with the ethical virtues is inherently good, it is also good for the sake of the contemplative life, and is what makes such a life possible. This is made clear in Aristotle's discussion

14 *Nicomachean Ethics* II.3, 1104b9-12.

of the state which is said to continue in existence "for the sake of a good life",[15] keeping in mind that the political life is one constituted by ethical virtue.

Although Aristotle refers to the contemplative life as being the most self-sufficient, he does not mean that people can or should withdraw from society. A person with philosophical wisdom will not need the same level of resources as an ethically virtuous person (they may even be a hindrance). As a composite being of form and matter, she cannot be detached either from society or the larger biological conditions of existence:

> Being connected with the passions also, the moral excellences must belong to our composite nature; and the excellences of our composite nature are human; so, therefore, are the life and the happiness which correspond to these. The excellence of the intellect is a thing apart; we must be content to say this much about it, for to describe it precisely is a task greater than our purpose requires. It would seem, however, also to need external equipment but little, or less than moral excellence does. *Grant that both need the necessaries, and do so equally, even if the statesman's work is the more concerned with the body and things of that sort; for there will be little difference there; but in what they need for the exercise of their activities there will be much difference*...for deeds many things are needed, and more, the greater and nobler the deeds are. But the man who is contemplating the truth needs no such thing, at least with a view to the exercise of his activity; indeed they are, one may say, even hindrances, at all events to his contemplation; *but in so far as he is a man and lives with a number of people, he chooses to do excellent acts*; he will therefore need such aids to living a human life[16] (my emphasis).

Not only do the ends of the two distinct forms of happiness differ,

---

15 *Politics* I.2, 1252b30.

16 *Nicomachean Ethics* X.8, 1178a19-28, 1178b1-7.

but so too their resource requirements. A goal of the ethically virtuous person is to practice the ethical virtues such as liberality, bravery, and justness. To exercise these virtues on a larger scale (making them greater and nobler) requires correspondingly greater resources. The ruler of a large city, for example, will need access to substantially greater resources to meet the city's needs, as compared to the head of a household and its needs. Both exercise virtue, but the ruler's activities are more noble because his deeds are more substantial. Contemplative activity, on the other hand, does not require the resources as noble moral activity, because it is not concerned with the practical necessities of our composite nature. Yet Aristotle makes clear that insofar as we are human and dependent upon social and environmental conditions, we **choose** to do excellent acts, because they are necessary to living a good human life.

Given our ability to bridge the gap between the composite world and that of form alone, we can engage in both kinds of activities. But since we are rooted in the composite world and have the same basic needs as any other mortal being, together with the corresponding responsibilities to uphold the greater good, individuals of good character will choose and take pleasure in exercising the practical virtues. As I interpret Aristotle, to lack a good character is to impede, if not eliminate, the possibility of leading the contemplative life. We should choose the practical virtues in part because they are inherently good, but primarily because they contribute to intellectual virtue:

> Now we call that which is in itself worthy of pursuit more complete than that which is worthy of pursuit for the sake of

> something else, and that which is never desirable for the sake of something else more complete than the things that are desirable both in themselves and for the sake of the other thing, and therefore we call complete without qualification that which is always desirable in itself and never for the sake of something else...every excellence we choose indeed for themselves (for if nothing resulted from them we should still choose each of them), but we choose them also for the sake of happiness, judging that through them we shall be happy.[17]

That contemplative activity is more complete than practical activity is made clear in X.7 where Aristotle says that contemplation "alone would seem to be loved for its own sake; for nothing arises from it apart from the contemplating, while from practical activities we gain more or less apart from the action".[18] This, I believe, is in keeping with a hierarchical conception of happiness that locates contemplative activity at the summit. As such, it is used as the target to guide our lives, but with the proviso that "complete happiness" cannot be achieved without all the other goods and activities instrumental or conducive to its realization.

Beyond self-sufficiency, there are other factors that contribute to the superiority of contemplation to deliberation. One such factor is the greater precision achievable in exercising theoretical as opposed to practical wisdom. As mentioned at the outset of the *Nicomachean Ethics*, practical considerations are subject to a great deal of fluctuation, and can only be addressed in outline.[19] Theoretical subjects, on the other hand, are more exacting, and address things that cannot

---

17 *Nicomachean Ethics* I.7, 1097a30-35, 1097b1-5.

18 *Nicomachean Ethics* X.7, 1177b1-3.

19 See *Nicomachean Ethics* I.4, 1094b12-27.

be otherwise.[20] Aristotle also considers the objects of understanding to be the best objects of knowledge, and to result in activity that is more continuous and pleasurable than any other.[21] All things considered, contemplative activity is superior because it is the best thing in us. In contemplating the fundamental truths of the world, we are mimicking the activity of God. By living a life as similar to God's as possible, we are living a life that is the happiest and most blessed for a human being. By extension, Aristotle believes that we should not content ourselves with living a purely human life, because we are not just human. Further, we should not limit our potential by being strictly concerned with human affairs and practical wisdom. Instead, we should "strain every nerve to live in accordance with the best thing in us," for in doing so, we come to realize our highest potential and satisfy our deepest desire. It is by understanding the world that we come to understand ourselves and our place in it. In the process, we come to realize the inherent goodness of the world, and our potential to either enhance or degrade that goodness.

PRACTICAL WISDOM AND ENVIRONMENTAL CONCERN

Since practical virtue is a prerequisite for intellectual virtue in that a philosopher must also be of good character, I want to examine the significance of environmental integrity from the perspective of the person having practical wisdom. The first consideration is that human beings are by nature political animals. As such, the ethically

[20] See *Metaphysics* I.2 for example.

[21] *Nicomachean Ethics* X.7, 1177a19-27.

virtuous person will not be found outside of society, since the virtues must be acquired through habituation and guidance that can only be found within society. For Aristotle, a man living outside the state is like an isolated checkers-piece with little hope for improvement:

> ...he who by nature and not by mere accident is without a state is either a bad man or above humanity. He is like the "tribeless, lawless, hearthless one" whom Homer denounces -- the natural outcast is forthwith a lover of war: he may be compared to an isolated piece at draughts.[22]

Aristotle is claiming that the very identity of a human is defined in terms of his or her relationship to society, and cannot be expressed outside society. From this perspective, the relationship of the state to an individual person is similar to that of a species and an individual organism, in that the whole is necessarily prior to the part.[23] If you destroy the state, then the individual will no more be a human being than a hand or foot will be such (except homonymously) if the body is destroyed. The existence of the individual is dependent upon the existence of the state in the same way as the existence of a hand or foot is dependent upon the existence of the entire organism. As described by Aristotle, the state is a natural entity that has developed in much the same way as an organism:

> When several villages are united in a single complete community, large enough to be nearly or quite self-sufficing, the state comes into existence, originating in the bare needs of life, and continuing in existence for the sake of a good life. And therefore,

---

[22] *Politics* I.2, 1253a2-6.

[23] *Politics* I.2, 1253a19-20.

> if the earlier forms of society are natural, so is the state, for it is the end of them, and the nature of a thing is its end. For what each thing is when fully developed, we call its nature, whether we are speaking of a man, a horse, or a family. Besides, the final cause and end of a thing is the best, and to be self-sufficing is the end and the best.[24]

As discussed earlier, Aristotle says that to have a nature is to have living form or soul. This indicates that a state too is a living entity, composed of human beings associating at different levels of organization from family to community. We thus appear to have a hierarchy of living form expressing a hierarchy of dependency of part to whole that includes the state.

Let us be clear that the state is also dependent upon the larger natural world for its existence. This is brought out in Aristotle's discussion of the acquisition of the various goods needed for life, for as he says, "no man can live well, or indeed live at all, unless he is provided with necessaries".[25] In the *Nicomachean Ethics*, Aristotle refers to the necessaries as consisting of three classes of goods described as being either external, of the soul, or of the body.[26] Whereas the *Nicomachean Ethics* was primarily concerned with goods relating to the soul, Aristotle was well aware that the good life could not be had in abstraction of the larger natural environment, given our dependency upon natural resources for survival. It is in the *Politics* that Aristotle discusses the implementation of the good life or the necessary conditions that must first be addressed before we can have any

[24] *Politics* I.2, 1252b28-1253a2.

[25] *Politics* I.4, 1253b25-26.

[26] *Nicomachean Ethics* I.8, 1098b11-14.

hope of living well.

In book I of the *Politics*, Aristotle begins to address the various ways in which our basic needs can be met through what he calls natural productive labor, or those that do not depend upon exchange or trade, such as shepherding, fishing and farming.[27] These modes of acquisition are given by nature to human beings as other modes are given to other creatures. It is in this context that Aristotle says that since nature produces nothing in vain, then it must be the case that she produces all things for the sake of man. As stated in chapter 2, this does not mean that other living things have no other value save as instruments for human utility. It is simply a statement that human beings are natural, and like other natural beings, we require resources for the sake of sustaining life. With respect to food, nature provides for all living things which may include other living beings, plant or animal. Since plants are utilized by animals, then they exist for the sake of animals. And since humans utilize other animals, then by extension other animals have been provided for the sake of humans. Nothing in this line of reasoning commits Aristotle to the idea that humans are the measure of all things. Instead, his reasoning can best be understood as the identification of ecological dependency.

Aristotle also speaks of getting property that is in accordance with nature as a part of household management. In this section, he describes true wealth as consisting of property that can be directly utilized for living a good life, as opposed to wealth accumulation. For Aristotle, true wealth is not limitless, despite the views of those

---

27 *Politics* I.8, 1256a40-1256b2.

claiming otherwise:

> Of the art of acquisition then there is one kind which by nature is a part of the management of a household, in so far as the art of household management must either find ready to hand, or itself provide, such things necessary to life, and useful for the community of the family or state, as can be stored. They are the elements of true riches; for the amount of property which is needed for a good life is not unlimited, although Solon in one of his poems says that 'No bound to riches has been fixed for man'. But there is a boundary fixed, just as there is in the other arts; for the instruments of any art are never unlimited, either in number or size, and riches may be defined as a number of instruments to be used in a household or in a state.[28]

Aristotle makes the case that true wealth is taken directly from nature and is important for life in society. Since wealth is defined in terms of instruments needed to lead a good life that are themselves limited, then the desire to acquire limitless wealth is misguided. This perspective is also reflected in the *Nicomachean Ethics* where Aristotle argues that happiness does not consist in wealth because it is useful only insofar as it contributes to the good life.[29] Anyone who considers happiness to consist in wealth is leading a vulgar life contrary to their own nature, because the point of household management is to use and distribute goods, not acquire them.[30] Further, the means that the household manager uses in order to acquire goods are aimed at living, and only a modest amount of goods is required for such an end.

---

28 *Politics* I.8, 1256b26-36.

29 *Nicomachean Ethics* I.5, 1096a6-8.

30 *Politics* I.9, 1257b31-2.

In stating that there are natural modes of resource acquisition, Aristotle is implying that there are unnatural modes as well. In fact, he discusses unnatural methods, and associates them with activities that are pursued beyond the satisfaction of needs such as results from trade and/or "money-making".[31] Part of his criticism of money-making ventures, like retail trade, is that the medium of exchange (i.e. money) has become divorced from the source of wealth from which it first arose as a substitute. In the process, people began to confuse wealth with money, and began to engage in activities aimed at acquiring ever more of these unnatural riches:

> Originating in the use of coin, the art of getting wealth is generally thought to be chiefly concerned with it, and to be the art which produces riches and wealth, having to consider how they may be accumulated. Indeed, riches is assumed by many to be only a quantity of coin, because the arts of getting wealth and retail trade are concerned with coin. Others maintain that coined money is a mere sham, a thing not natural, but conventional only, because, if the users substitute another commodity for it, it is worthless, and because it is not useful as a means to any of the necessities of life, and, indeed, he who is rich in coin may often be in want of necessary food. But how can that be wealth of which a man may have a great abundance and yet perish with hunger, like Midas in the fable, whose insatiable prayer turned everything that was set before him into gold? Hence men seek after a better notion of riches and of the art of getting wealth, and they are right.[32]

How can money constitute wealth if a man can have it in abundance, yet still starve for lack of food? By focusing on money and material acquisition, we are being blinded to the real source of wealth and

[31] *Politics* I.9.

[32] *Politics* I.9, 1257b5-19.

riches: nature herself.

In this discussion of the acquisition of goods I am reminded of Aldo Leopold and his criticism of the idea of progress with its emphasis on materialism:

> ...our bigger-and-better society is now like a hypochondriac, so obsessed with its own economic health as to have lost the capacity to remain healthy. The whole world is so greedy for more bathtubs that it has lost the stability necessary to build them, or even to turn off the tap. Nothing could be more salutary at this stage than a little healthy contempt for a plethora of material blessings.[33]

Leopold was concerned not only that we had a dysfunctional conception of progress, but also that we had lost touch with the natural world by not appreciating the source of our material blessings. As he says, two of the spiritual dangers of not being a farmer are "...the danger of supposing that breakfast comes from the grocer", and "... that heat comes from the furnace".[34] By focusing on material accumulation, people are missing the point of living well, and also failing to see the source of true wealth.

Although Aristotle may not have explicitly addressed the possibility of environmental problems, it should now be obvious that he recognized the importance of natural resources in supplying humans with the necessary means to live a good life. Given that the function of the state is to provide the conditions for a good life for all citizens, and since the state was dependent upon natural resources

---

33 Leopold, 1966: Xix.

34 Ibid., p. 6

for its well-being, then it stands to reason that anything interfering with needs satisfaction and the stability of the state (such as environmental degradation) would have generated great concern. Since we are naturally gregarious, our individual stability and security is directly tied to the stability and security of society. This helps to explain why Aristotle was so concerned with the "greater good" and how the well-being of society as a whole was more important than that of an individual. If it is true that society is dependent upon the natural world in the same way that humans are dependent upon society, then environmental integrity has an even greater claim for its preservation than that of society. But to address this question adequately, it will be necessary to go beyond practical considerations, and begin to explore the metaphysical basis for environmental preservation.

THE LIFE OF CONTEMPLATION AND THE CONTEMPLATION OF LIFE

Human beings can be defined in two ways, articulating two modes of existence. The first is as composites of form and matter found in the world of everyday experience. This is the world we encounter through our senses, and is foundational to satisfying our desire to know or understand. Human form in this mode is maintained by activities aimed at the perpetuation of the species-form, such as nutrition and reproduction, given the perishable nature of our composite existence. The second is as human soul consisting of form alone, and representing our highest level of actuality. In this world, we abstract form from matter through the activity of contemplation. In doing so, we not only come to understand what it is to be human, but also what it is to be any living being. By exercising our minds, we engage in the same activity as the unmoved mover, and connect with an element within us that is both eternal and divine.

These modes of existence make it possible to consider two ways in which humans can become happy. As animal composites of form and matter, we can realize partial happiness through ethically virtuous activity. Practical deliberation may not lead to complete happiness, but we will be living in a way that at least approximates the best of lives. As form without matter, we can become completely happy through philosophically virtuous activity, because we will be adhering to the absolute standard of happiness (i.e. the eternal contemplative activity of God). Through contemplation, we transcend the strictly human life as a perishable composite, and live the life that is happiness itself. At the base of each life is a commitment to excellence to live a life that is best either for a human to lead (i.e. ethically virtuous) or simply best (i.e. philosophically virtuous).

This line of reasoning emerges from Aristotle's teleology as life seeks to actualize form. Growth and development of organisms, for example, was explained in terms of the end for the sake of which it occurred – a mature and normally active organism. This makes the world full of potentiality and actuality corresponding to the extent form has been realized.[35] Human form can exist at different levels of actuality, corresponding to the level of understanding achieved as a consequence of our innate desire to know. And it is only by way

[35] See *On the Soul* II.5, 417a22-417b1.

of actively contemplating the essences found in the world that we come to fully actualize our form by satisfying our desire to know,[36] and live the life that is happiest.[37] The possibility of having knowledge about the world is realized by its ultimate intelligibility. Unlike other species, humans are capable of receiving the intelligible forms found in the world in abstraction of their material circumstances.[38] But before we can understand the world we must first make the effort to experience it through observation and study as part of natural philosophy.[39] Herein lies the importance of environmental integrity from a metaphysical perspective, at least with respect to the preservation of biodiversity. Without sensible things in the world existing in a way dictated by the natural expression of species-form, then it becomes impossible for us to adequately understand the world and thus satisfy our desire to know.

The significance of environmental integrity is ultimately rooted in the objective goodness found in the world, both as a systematic whole, and as embodied in individual organisms. With respect to the goodness found in the world as a whole, Aristotle clearly finds it in God and the order that God brings to the world.[40] The order of the world is brought to it by God in the same way that a leader brings order to an army. In this description of the goodness of the universe,

[36] *On the Soul* II.5, 417a28-9.

[37] *Nicomachean Ethics* X.7,1177b27-1178a8.

[38] *On the Soul* III.4, 429a13-17.

[39] *On the Soul* III.8, 432a4-9.

[40] *Metaphysics* XII.10, 1075a11-19.

we encounter the paradigmatic relationship of part to whole. In the same way that an individual human is defined in terms of her relationship to society, all other beings are ordered together and defined in terms of their relationship to the whole universe made possible by God. It is this relationship of part to whole that gives priority to environmental integrity considered as a systematic whole to that of any subordinate part, whether as an individual or community.

All things are ultimately dependent upon God, because it is through God's thinking that the actuality of existence is secured. Remember that Aristotle argued that there must be a prior actuality of all forms in order for anything to exist by nature, even if only potentially. That prior actuality is made possible through God's thinking, because thought and the object of thought are one and the same.[41] By thinking the world as a whole, God is giving actuality to the world as a whole, because God thinking *is* the world. That is why Aristotle referred to God as a living being:

> And life also belongs to God; for the actuality of thought is life, and God is that actuality; and God's essential actuality is life most good and eternal. We say therefore that God is a living being, eternal, most good, so that life and duration continuous and eternal belong to God; for this *is* God.[42]

Therein lies the basis for Aristotle's claim that the world is a good place. It is objectively good for "life [that is God] is most good and eternal". To have life is to share in the goodness of God.

CONCLUSION

[41] *Metaphysics* XII.7, 1072b20-22.

[42] *Metaphysics* XII.7, 1072b26-31.

Aristotle considered virtuous human beings to be superior to other forms of life on earth, since we are able to approximate more closely the life of God, and therefore exhibit a greater share of God's goodness. But in order to satisfy our desire to understand the world, we must actively encounter form and matter as manifested in the variety of species and communities of life that exist in the realm of experience.[43] Without sense information, we have no hope of ever learning or understanding anything, because the mind is not able to take on the intelligible forms of things in abstraction of sensible form. It is this line of reasoning that propels Aristotle to engage in an active defense of his biological studies, and which leads him to conclude that all life, however ignoble, is a source of wonder and beauty.[44]

I want also to point out that desire can be analyzed from two different perspectives emerging from the world's ultimate intelligibility. On the one hand, life on Earth manifests a desire to understand the world as exhibited by an innate curiosity among those creatures having mind (i.e. human beings), who are filled with wonder and puzzlement and seek to determine the "why" of things.[45] On the other hand, life also manifests a desire to be understood to the extent that all sensible form has projective power. When we sense a scarlet tanager for example, it is the sensible form "Scarlet Tanager" that is impressing itself onto our sense faculty in the same way that

---

43 *On the Soul* III.8, 432a7-9.

44 *Parts of Animals* I.5, 645a4-25.

45 In *Metaphysics* I.2, 982b13-14, Aristotle says, "...it is owing to their wonder that men both now begin and at first began to philosophize..."

a signet ring impresses its shape onto wax.[46] By reducing our ability to encounter life's variety, either as individual organisms or in ecological association, we are foreclosing opportunities for both understanding and self-understanding – two aspects of the principle cause of good in the world.[47]

That we currently live in a world that is willing to accept environmental destruction and biological impoverishment in the name of progress, with such little remorse or misgiving, may be the expected consequence of a species unable to act in accordance with its nature. Like other living beings, we are natural because we have soul, or an inner principle of change directed at the realization of our species-specific form as part of the universal form that is God. We differ from other beings in that the organization of our desires does not arise within us by nature, but must be molded by others in society through habituation (the ethical virtues) and teaching (the philosophical virtues). Since so few people are apparently able to fulfill their nature and thus live a life according to nature, we can begin to understand why the impetus of human society has been moving contrary to nature. The question that should have troubled

46 *On the Soul* II.12, 424a17-24. As mentioned previously, this is not to imply that nonhuman organisms depend upon human beings to realize fully their potential as beings having form. Understanding or self-understanding does not constitute part of the essence of those species lacking mind (although existence as such is made possible because of God's eternal understanding). The point is only that the formal nature of things exhibits a projective power that can affect impressionable minds through sense perception, and that once the form of something is brought to mind, what is understanding for the contemplator is self-understanding for the form being contemplated since thought and the object of thought are one and the same.

47 *Metaphysics* I.2, 982a30-b10.

Aristotle more than it seems is why the good life is so evasive? Why are we so inept at being human?

NOTES

Jonathan Lear, *Aristotle: The Desire to Understand,* (New York: Cambridge University Press, 1988).

Aldo Leopold, *A Sand County Almanac: With Other Essays on Conservation from Round River,* (New York: Random House, 1966).

CHAPTER 5: FRIENDSHIP, SELF-LOVE AND BIOPHILIA

INTRODUCTION

In chapters 8 and 9 of the *Nicomachean Ethics*, Aristotle discusses the importance of friendship. A justification for addressing this topic emerges from his assertion that an individual living in isolation would be unable to achieve success in life. This is because the resources needed to develop the virtues and participate in the intellectual life can be realized only within a socially rich environment. Friends are important for the virtuous man in part because of their instrumental value in becoming successful. Being a social animal, we need interaction with others of good character in order to become good ourselves. But Aristotle is not claiming that the value of friends is exhausted by their usefulness to us as a means to an end. As I interpret these two chapters, his primary emphasis is to show why we should value our friends for their own sake. In fact, Aristotle indicates that in specific circumstances, self-sacrifice may be required to preserve the well-being of friends.

The question I want to address in this chapter is whether his ideas on friendship can be extended to include nonhumans. In particular, I want to determine if we as human beings could have a justifiable reason to benefit the nonhuman world sharing our earthly domain for their own sake in something like friendship. Since Aristotle did not consider this possibility himself, I will attempt to build such an argument consistent with his philosophical thought. I begin by reviewing Aristotle's conception of friendship and its relationship to self-love.

This will allow me to speculate on the moral basis for considering the well-being of the nonhuman world for reasons not exhausted by their instrumentality. In other words, I will attempt to offer an Aristotelian account of the inherent value of the living world.

THE NATURE OF FRIENDSHIP

In IX.4 of the *Nicomachean Ethics*, Aristotle lists five characteristics of friendship. To be a friend to another, one must: (1) wish and do good for a friend for his sake, (2) wish his friend to live and exist for his own sake, (3) wish to associate with his friend, (4) live the same kind of life as his friend, and (5) share the same pleasures and pains as his friend. This list makes clear that an active association is a key ingredient of friendship given that Aristotle thought we should not only share the same kind of life as our friends, but ***do*** good for them for their sake. One must be willing to go beyond simply wishing a friend well, but be willing to act on their behalf so they too may become successful. The beneficent nature of friendship is articulated by Aristotle when he distinguishes friendship from goodwill:

> Goodwill is a friendly sort of relation, but is not *identical* with friendship; for one may have goodwill both towards people whom one does not know, and without their knowing it, but not friendship. This has indeed been said already. But goodwill is not even friendly feeling. For it does not involve intensity or desire, whereas these accompany friendly feeling; and friendly feeling implies intimacy while goodwill may arise of a sudden, as it does towards competitors in a contest; we come to feel goodwill for them and to share in their wishes, but we would not *do* anything with them; for, as we said, we feel goodwill suddenly and love them only superficially.[1]

1 *Nicomachean Ethics* IX.5, 1166b30-1167a2.

When exhibiting goodwill toward someone, we ***wish*** them well but ***do*** nothing for them. Although it is necessary to have goodwill toward another in order to establish a friendly relationship, friendship itself expresses a much deeper level of intimacy than is captured by goodwill.[2] In addition to wishful regard, there must also exist a shared concern for the other person, drawn from a prolonged period of close association. Apparently, Aristotle thought that only through shared and enduring experiences do friends feel compelled to benefit each other for their own sakes. Although we may take pleasure in the presence of strangers and wish them well, the desire to act on their behalf is lacking.

In saying that goodwill involves a superficial love for another, Aristotle is thus asserting that friendship involves a much more substantial loving relationship. In fact, he states that friendship seems to lie in loving rather than in being loved, since some can take pleasure in the good fortune of others even when they do not or cannot expect their love to be returned.[3] Such is the case, Aristotle believes, for mothers acting in the best interest of their children by giving them into the care of others. As long as her children prosper, then it does not matter to a mother that she also be loved by them, for her satisfaction is found in doing well by them for their own sake.

To modern readers, describing the parent-child relationship as one of friendship may seem odd. Perhaps something has been lost in the translation from the Greek that does not quite capture the

2 *Nicomachean Ethics* IX.5, 1167a3.

3 *Nicomachean Ethics* VIII.8, 1159a26.

nature of the concept being addressed.[4] But that Aristotle considered a loving relationship between differing classes of people to be possible, such as that of parent and child, there can be no doubt. At the very beginning of his discussion, he even mentions that friendship can occur among birds and most animals.[5] Although Aristotle claims that equality is a characteristic of friendship,[6] he nevertheless acknowledges that it may also exist in relationships that are not equal.

SELF-LOVE

In IX.8 Aristotle asks whether a man should love himself most of all, or someone else. Although many people have apparently examined this section with an eye toward determining if Aristotle was an egoist,[7] my interest is focused more on the relationship of self-love to his larger ethical and metaphysical viewpoint.[8] In my interpretation, self-love is of fundamental importance for the person seeking to live well. If one does not love one's self, then there is no basis for friendship, nor hope for happiness. To put self-love into perspective, Aristotle says the following:

4 Annas, *Self-Love in Aristotle* (1989) has expressed her dissatisfaction with the term "friendship" as being an adequate translation (although she does not suggest an alternative).

5 *Nicomachean Ethics* VIII.1, 1155a16-20.

6 *Nicomachean Ethics* VIII.7, 1158b24-28.

7 Annas, 1989.

8 Kraut (1989) provides a convincing argument that Aristotle was not an egoist in any meaningful way.

> The question is also debated, whether a man should love himself most, or some one else. People criticize those who love themselves most, and call them self-lovers, using this as an epithet of disgrace, and a bad man seems to do everything for his own sake, and the more so the more wicked he is - and so men reproach him, for instance, with doing nothing of his own accord -while the good man acts for honour's sake, and the more so the better he is, and acts for his friend's sake, and sacrifices his own interest. But the facts clash with these arguments, and this is not surprising. For men say that one ought to love best one's best friend, and a man's best friend is one who wishes well to the object of his wish for his sake, even if no one is to know of it; and these attributes are found most of all in a man's attitude towards himself...[9]

Aristotle is here casting doubt upon the common conception of self-love, for it would appear that we are our own best friend in that we wish well for ourselves most of all. This suggests that friendship is not strictly altruistic, given that our actions toward others are not completely selfless. There is something about our own selves that is worthy of deep respect - providing the template for the type of regard we should extend to our friends.

Aristotle subsequently explains that a self-lover, properly conceived, identifies "self" in terms of the most authoritative element of his being.[10] He argues that the problem with common conceptions of self-love is that "self" is defined in terms of one's corporeal and uniquely individual person. Self-love then often becomes expressed in terms of selfishness and the satisfaction of selfish desires. Since most people have unorganized souls and do not desire the things they ought, then they fail to recognize and love the best

9 *Nicomachean Ethics* IX.8, 1168a28-b4.

10 *Nicomachean Ethics* IX.8, 1168b31-33.

part of themselves - seeking instead to satisfy unguided individual appetites. On the other hand, A true self-lover identifies "self" with that part of soul representing his true nature. Properly conceived, a self-lover loves his understanding most of all and not his discrete individual and composite being. In loving his understanding, he obeys and gratifies the authoritative element of human soul:

> ...such a man would seem more than the other a lover of self; at all events he assigns to himself the things that are noblest and best, and gratifies the most authoritative element in himself and in all things obeys this; and just as a city or any other systematic whole is most properly identified with the most authoritative element in it, so is a man; and therefore the man who loves this and gratifies it is most of all a lover of self.[11]

Aristotle is thus defining "self" in terms consistent with human nature. It is a mistake to call grasping and selfish individuals self-lovers, for they do not obey the authoritative element within them as human beings. Living lives contrary to their own nature, they have no recognition of their humanity. Therefore, how can it be meaningful to describe such irrational people as lovers of self?

I think it also clear that Aristotle considered a genuine self-lover to be concerned primarily with the common good, and not with his own individual well-being:

> Those, then, who busy themselves in an exceptional degree with noble actions all men approve and praise; and if all were to strive towards what is noble and strain every nerve to do the noblest deeds, everything would be as it should be for the common good, and every one would secure for himself the goods

11 *Nicomachean Ethics* IX.8, 1168b29-34.

> that are greatest, since excellence is the greatest of goods.[12]

By stating that everyone should secure for themselves the goods that are greatest, Aristotle could be interpreted as telling people to be selfish, but in an unusual way. It is as if we are to be engaged in what Kraut[13] refers to as "moral competition", in which the object is to exhibit a greater level of virtue than others. Heroism, for example, may be interpreted as a means to secure a greater good for oneself (i.e. nobility), than would be given to others who might benefit from a heroic deed (i.e. saving a life). As Aristotle says, it is better to live a short life of intense pleasure than to live a long life of mild enjoyment.[14] But it should be kept in mind that the object of one's selfish desire in this instance is virtue. A good person takes heroic action for the sake of virtue, not for the sake of being a hero. In doing what virtue requires of a good man, he is showing the proper love of self. This is the case since it is the love of understanding generally, and not that of any particular individual, that is the object of desire.

BENEVOLENT-REGARD

To explore the possible justification for human beings acting on behalf of the nonhuman world, it is necessary to consider the variety of friendly relationships that exist among members of different and unequal groups. Clearly, we cannot characterize the relationship between humans and the rest of the natural world as embodying

12 *Nicomachean Ethics* IX.8, 1169a6-11.

13 Kraut, 1989, Chapter 2.

14 *Nicomachean Ethics* IX.8, 1169a21-25.

friendship, since it is not based upon mutual love (at least not in a strict sense). I think it demonstrably true that some people actively engage in efforts aimed at ensuring the well-being of an assortment of natural entities (from animals to ecosystems) for their own sake, and without the expectation of receiving anything in return. Because of their active regard for non-human beings, it goes well beyond what could be described as expressing goodwill. So it would appear that if we want to adequately characterize the relationship between humans and the nonhuman world, then we need a term and relationship that goes beyond goodwill, but is not based upon mutual affection.

For the sake of discussion, I will refer to this type of concern as benevolent-regarding behavior, and will categorize friendship as a form of benevolent-regard that occurs among people. This, I think, is consistent with Aristotle's perspective on the limits of friendship:

> ...it is not possible to define exactly up to what point friends can remain friends; for much can be taken away and friendship remain, but when one party is removed to a great distance, as God is, the possibility of friendship ceases.[15]

Our arms are too short to hug God, so to speak. But neither can we become friends with beings on the other side of the hierarchical dividing line, since Aristotle also claims that friendship can't be extended toward a horse or an ox.[16] Yet, with respect to our relationship to God, I interpret Aristotle as saying elsewhere that virtuous

---

15 *Nicomachean Ethics* VII.7, 1159a2-5.

16 *Nicomachean Ethics* VIII.11, 1161b2-3.

people still have responsibilities derived from the debt owed to God for making life possible. We are indebted to God, as we are to our parents, beyond our ability to adequately compensate - although as discussed later, we must do what we can. And if virtue dictates that we have a responsibility to superior beings, does it not also require some measure of responsibility or active interest in the welfare of inferior beings (e.g. other biological species)?

To provide a firmer footing for this argument, it would be useful to find some basis for determining the proper expression of benevolent-regard among beings of unequal merit or ability, thereby giving us a standard for relating to beings of superior (i.e. God) or inferior (i.e. other animals) worth. Fortunately, a possible outline for this strategy is reflected in Aristotle's discussion of the kind of friendship that may exist between people of different class. According to Aristotle, love among friends involving an inequality such as that occurring between father and son or elder to younger, should be proportional to the inequality of the relationship:

> In all friendships implying inequality the love also should be proportional, i.e. the better should be more loved than he loves, and so should the more useful, and similarly in each of the other cases; for when the love is in proportion to the merit of the parties, then in a sense arises equality, which is held to be characteristic of friendship.[17]

Since Aristotle believes that equality is a characteristic of friendship, there must be a means whereby a level of equality can be achieved that can bridge the difference between parties. His answer is that

17 *Nicomachean Ethics* VIII.7, 1158b24-28.

we should love others in proportion to their merit. This equation suggests that apportioning love is like apportioning justice. The friend who is better or more successful should be loved more than the friend who is less successful.

That love can be apportioned in a way that satisfies principles of justice is made explicit in Aristotle's discussion of friendship as it exists between ruler and ruled. According to Aristotle, if there is no justice, there can be no friendship:

> Each of the constitutions may be seen to involve friendship just in so far as it involves justice ... The friendship of man and wife... is the same that is found in an aristocracy; for it is in accordance with excellence – the better gets more of what is good, and each gets what befits him; and so, too, with the justice in these relations ... But in the deviation-forms, as justice hardly exists, so too does friendship. It exists least in the worst form; in tyranny there is little or no friendship. For where there is nothing common to ruler and ruled, there is not friendship either, since there is not justice...[18]

This was the basis for his saying that there could be no friendship between men and other animals. Since the distance between the two parties is so great, there can be no justice between them, and thus no basis for friendship.

Although Aristotle states that superior people should be accorded more love than their inferiors, I do not interpret this to mean that superiors should receive more of all things in all situations. His underlying theme throughout his discussion of friendship is that one should always seek a proportionate response relative to each situation. In following this prescription, the aim is to equalize disparate

[18] *Nicomachean Ethics* VIII.11, 1161a10-11, 22-25, 30-33.

relationships as much as possible. This is illustrated by an example he provides in relations between friends of unequal wealth, one of whom has more than he needs, the other less.[19] Aristotle says that each should get more out of the friendship, but not more of the same thing. The person in need should be given more of his friend's wealth whereas the benefactor should be given more honor. Each reward is appropriate to the circumstances - honor for virtue and assistance for need as a means to preserve the friendship. This is necessary because not all parties are in the position to repay debts in the same measure as they were received:

> This then is also the way in which we should associate with unequals; the man who is benefitted in respect of wealth or excellence must give honour in return, repaying what he can. For friendship asks a man to do what he can, not what is proportional to the merits of the case; since that cannot always be done, e.g. in honours paid to the gods or to parents; for no one could ever return to them the equivalent of what he gets, but the man who serves them to the utmost of his power is thought to be a good man.[20]

As mentioned previously, Aristotle thought friendship is built upon something held in common by each party. The truest friendship is based upon mutual recognition of goodwill among people of good character.[21] It is the goodness of each person that is both loved and desired between friends, and is what each share in common. By loving his friend, a man of good character is loving both what

---

19 *Nicomachean Ethics* VIII.14, 11631b1-4.

20 *Nicomachean Ethics* VIII.14, 1163b13-18.

21 *Nicomachean Ethics* VIII.4, 1157a30-32.

is good for himself, and what is good for his friend in so far as all good men need friends. He is also loving his "self" most of all because what makes his friend good is his understanding -- an activity shared by all people of good character. It is from this perspective that Aristotle says that a friend is another self.[22] But there are also relationships that strain the basis for friendship, in that the differences between the parties far exceed what is shared in common. In such situations, considerations of justice are inapplicable. It may be impossible, for example, to return anything approaching equivalence to what has been received. Such is the case for the debts we owe to the gods and to our parents, for no one can adequately compensate what has been received from either source (i.e. life itself). That is why Aristotle states that we should honor both the gods and our parents, no matter what the circumstance.

But what is interesting to me in the quote above is that there remains an implied moral relationship between beings whose differences are so great that the basis for friendship has been exceeded - such as our relationship to God. But what about our association to other life that also exceeds the parameters of friendship? May we not have reason to behave in a morally appropriate way to the perishable nonhuman world, for example? If so, what would be the basis for our relationship? Of additional interest is Aristotle's claim that there are situations in which we can benefit another without expecting anything in return. It is not always necessary or realistic to expect or demand some form of repayment for acts of assistance.

22 *Nicomachean Ethics* IX.3, 1166a30-32.

In fact, Aristotle says that benefactors can receive a great deal just for engaging in beneficent activity.[23] This is because we are what we do. A good life is one lived in accordance with virtue with virtuous activity being its own reward. Thus, one can benefit another and not care whether an equivalent action is returned, given the inherent goodness of virtuous activity itself. Mothers, for example, take delight in seeing their children prosper "even if these owing to their ignorance give them nothing of a mother's due".[24]

We therefore appear to have two related threads to examine in our account of the proper expression of benevolent-regard towards the nonhuman world. The first is derived from the responsibility (if any) that virtuous individuals may have toward the rest of the natural world, for which the dictates of justice do not apply. The second is derived from the desire to live in accordance with virtue. Aristotle says that, in seeking to fulfill our responsibility to others, we should strive to do what is appropriate under the circumstances, and to compare the claims between parties according to such factors as nearness of relation, excellence, or utility. Although this may not be easy, Aristotle adds that "we must not on *that* account shrink from the task, but decide the question as best we can".[25]

23 *Nicomachean Ethics* IX.7, 1167b17-1168a9.

24 *Nicomachean Ethics* VIII.8, 1159a31-32. Does this not commit Aristotle to admitting that friendship need not be of a reciprocal nature?

25 *Nicomachean Ethics* IX.2, 1165a30-36.

MORAL RESPONSIBILITY AND THE NONHUMAN WORLD

If there is to be a basis for human moral responsibility toward the nonhuman natural world, then we must look to Aristotle's account of how unequals are to interact. According to Aristotle, unequals should render in honor or benefits what is in proportion to their relative superiority or inferiority.[26] Although he was primarily, if not exclusively, concerned with the equality or inequality of inter-human relationships, his formula appears to be applicable at all levels of existence. He says, for example, that honors are to be paid to the gods in virtue of our indebtedness to them. If we can also have good reason to behave in a morally appropriate way to nonhuman inferiors, in proportion to what they are due (if they are due anything), then how would this be derived and manifested?

I would like to offer the following speculative outline, to serve as a framework for conceiving our moral relationship to other species as members of the biotic community. I want to broaden the horizons that Aristotle developed in his discussion of the human good in society. In a sense, I am attempting to accomplish the same task that Leopold set for himself in developing the land ethic in terms of biotic citizenship. Whereas Leopold maintained human beings were but plain members and citizens of the biotic community, an Aristotelian approach would surely not be so egalitarian, given the hierarchical arrangement Aristotle perceived to be the order of life. Yet it is clear to me that he considered human beings to be members of a much larger community than that of the *polis*. We may be political ani-

26 *Nicomachean Ethics* VIII.13, 1162b4.

mals and naturally gregarious, but we are animals nonetheless. Our existence goes beyond the confines of society, and is inextricably embedded in the broader environment.

In our dealings with other people, our obligations seem to be fairly straight-forward if not precisely determinable insofar as we share much in common. But in our dealings with other species or ecosystems, the matter gets complicated, as there are many different species embodying different levels of association in various forms of ecological community. Clearly, our relationship to nonhuman life would not be defined in the same terms as for God or virtuous people, but I am persuaded that some moral consideration can reasonably be accorded the rest of the natural world in an Aristotelian worldview. My claim will draw from two Aristotelian assumptions or principles: (1) all life embodies an element of the divine either as a part (i.e. an individual organism) or as a systematic whole (i.e. a species, ecosystem, or cosmos) making it inherently valuable; and (2) nonhuman life is instrumentally valuable for the virtuous human being.

With respect to the first factor, Aristotle maintains that life is an expression of desire for God, in that the prior actuality of form is realized through divine contemplation. Form in turn is both the cause of change for living things, and the end for the sake of which all living things exist. Since thought and the object of thought are considered by Aristotle to be one and the same, in striving to realize their form at its highest level of actuality, all living beings are drawn toward self-understanding. Unfortunately, self-understanding is beyond the capacity of most animals, due to their lack of an intellectual faculty. Human beings alone, among perishable creatures of form and matter, are blessed with mind, and are therefore able to engage in rational activity. This was the basis for Aristotle's claim that human beings are superior to the other species of life on Earth, and why no other mortal being can ever partake in happiness.

Understanding is what the self-lover loves most of all, because it more than anything else is "self", being the authoritative and better part of all human beings. Yet Aristotle also indicates that understanding is a divine activity, surpassing anything of value in the purely human realm:

> If mind is divine, then, in comparison with man, the life according to it is divine in comparison with human life. But we must not follow those who advise us, being men, to think of human things, and, being mortal, of mortal things, but must, so far as we can, make ourselves immortal, and strain every nerve to live in accordance with the best thing in us; for even if it be small in bulk, much more does it in power and worth surpass everything.[27]

This leads to the curious perspective that a uniquely human life may not be purely human at all. This is the case because, to fulfill our true nature, we must actually seek to live a life that is divine. Self-understanding is therefore an understanding not so much of the human self as of the divine self. Thus, when we love our self most of all, we are not loving something that is unique to human life - we are loving that which moves all things, including other species of life.

That there is a divine element in all other living things is indicated by Aristotle when offering a defense of biological studies:

[27] *Nicomachean Ethics* X.7, 1177b30-1178a1.

> We ... must not recoil with childish aversion from the examination of the humbler animals. Every realm of nature is marvelous: and as Heraclitus, when the strangers who came to visit him found him warming himself at the furnace in the kitchen and hesitated to go in, is reported to have bidden them not to be afraid to enter, *as even in that kitchen divinities were present*, so we should venture on the study of every kind of animal without distaste; for each and all will reveal to us something natural and something beautiful (my emphasis).[28]

On my reading, Aristotle is claiming that all living things embody a divine element as part of their nature. Although the non-human world may not have the capacity to engage in rational activity, they still have a share of the divine. This I think reflects his conclusion that all life is dependent upon and expresses a desire for God, in that all living things strive to partake in the divine in so far as they are able.[29] For most life on Earth, this involves activities that seek to ensure the perpetuation of the species. Through such activities, mortal beings are assured of eternal existence "not as the self-same individual but... in something like itself -- not numerically but specifically one".[30]

I also understand Aristotle to be saying that the order of the world as a whole is an expression of desire for God. This is brought out in the *Metaphysics* where he says that all things are connected and share for the good of the whole.[31] And in the *Nicomachean Ethics*, he says that each thing, whether a man, a city, or any other systematic whole is identified with the most authoritative element

28 *Parts of Animals* I.5, 645a15-23.

29 *On the Soul* II.4, 415a30-b1.

30 *On the Soul* II.4, 415b6-8.

31 *Metaphysics* XII.10, 1075a15-24.

within it.[32] Since reality is constituted by God's actively thinking the world as a whole, then it must be that understanding is the authoritative element that defines existence as such. Given that a self-lover loves his understanding most of all, can he not also love the rest of the world that is the manifestation of God's understanding?

I think we have reason to answer in the affirmative, for benevolent-regard does not involve a love of self in an egoistic sense, nor is it a love of human life in an anthropocentric sense. Rather, benevolent-regard embodies an active and loving regard toward God insofar as God's thinking the world is the basis for reality. A true self-lover is one who loves the element within him that is both authoritative and divine. Since all friends of good character not only share but are guided by this same element, then we can meaningfully say that a friend is another self. And when we act on our friends' behalf for their own sake or for no other reason than that they should benefit, then we are also acting in a way consistent with self-love.

I should point out that understanding is not only the cause of human growth and development (since all men by nature desire to know) and that for the sake of which growth and development occurs (since perfect happiness consists in contemplation), but also the force that moves all life. It is for this reason that Aristotle refers to God as the unmoved mover, for he moves things without himself being moved. Aristotle is not implying that God created the world, or that the cosmos is God's handiwork. Rather, life is sustained by God's thinking the world, and is a response to that thinking which

32 *Nicomachean Ethics* IX.8, 1168b31-33.

has existed eternally. It is God's understanding that establishes the prior actuality of all living things, from part to whole, and serves as both the end of existence and the cause of movement. Even though the various other living beings are incapable of contemplation (and therefore of happiness) their growth and development is nonetheless driven by the same desire that motivates human beings to live virtuously. It must be the case then that all uncorrupted living beings embody some measure of the divine self that forms the basis of friendship. And if this is true, then there is no reason to believe that we cannot also be expected to express some level of benevolent-regard or love toward non-human nature, in a manner appropriate to the circumstances. The implications of this interpretation are that our love for understanding can encompass a love for all things fulfilling their nature from the least appealing of individual creatures, to the world as a whole insofar as each is good.[33]

With respect to the second factor, Aristotle indicates that what is good and pleasant in itself is also good for the virtuous human being.[34] That is why he said that we should have friends:

> If, then, existence is in itself desirable for the blessed man (since

---

[33] I do not interpret this as saying that everything in the world is good, and thus everything in the world is to be loved. Insofar as each thing we encounter in the world of everyday experience is a manifestation of the Good (i.e. lives according to its nature), then it is to be respected in a way appropriate to the circumstances. For example, we should love good people (not all people) because they are good, not because they exist. It is their understanding that is the basis for our friendship, not their existence. Good people have properly fulfilled their nature by living a life according to virtue. Unlike most, they have organized their desires so that they desire nothing amiss and do not live contrary to their nature.

[34] *Nicomachean Ethics* IX.9, 1170a20-22.

> it is by its nature good and pleasant), and that of his friend is very much the same, a friend will be one of the things that are desirable. Now that which is desirable for him he must have, or he will be deficient in this respect. The man who is to be happy will therefore need virtuous friends.[35]

Friends and other living beings are desirable in part because being conscious of things good in themselves is also inherently good and pleasant. At a more basic level, I take Aristotle to be implying that we should be concerned with maintaining environmental integrity, for life itself is a prerequisite for the good life. We value our existence, and find life to be pleasurable and good in itself, but being perishable beings, we must equip ourselves with all the various external goods that are necessary not just for living, but for living well.

Beyond our fundamental need for food, material, and labor, nonhuman nature is also a source of perceptible form. Without the ability to perceive form, we would be unable to render the living world intelligible by bringing form to mind. Since form is a component of life as such, we should be sensitive to the existence and well-being of all species (not just those of direct instrumental value) in our efforts to understand the world. Given that species do not exist in a vacuum, part of our task will be the effort to understand the world in a holistic way, since species are enmeshed with other species and the abiotic world. This being the case, our understanding of the world as a whole is only as rich as the world is diverse. The important point is that none of our needs can be had in abstraction of our environmental circumstances. We depend utterly upon what

[35] *Nicomachean Ethics* IX.9, 1170b14-18.

nature provides in order to have any hope of achieving happiness, whether our concern is directed toward what Aristotle refers to as goods of the body, goods of the soul, or external goods.

Beyond any moral consideration due to the nonhuman world, I do not think it unreasonable to act on their behalf for their sake without the expectation of getting anything in return. Annas[36] interprets Aristotle as saying that we are equipped with feelings of affinity for ourselves and for our offspring, and after the development of reason, we come to extend concern toward others.[37] Although our concern for the well-being of nonhumans may be based, at least initially, more on instinct than reason, our concern can also be explained and defended rationally. In the same way that mothers love their offspring and make sacrifices for their sake even if their love is not returned, we can also make sacrifices for the sake of nonhuman beings that are the objects of our benevolent-regard, who cannot consciously give anything in return.

The cause of such action is rooted in the nature of our existence:

> The cause of this is that existence is to all men a thing to be chosen and loved, and that we exist by virtue of activity (i.e. by living and acting), and that the handiwork *is* in a sense, the producer in activity; he loves his handiwork, therefore, because he loves existence. And this is rooted in the nature of things; for

....

36 Annas, 1989, 3.

37 It would appear that Aristotle is not quite right in that we also seem to be equipped with feelings of affinity for many other animals as well. In a discussion of neoteny, Gould (*The Panda's Thumb*) relates how people are naturally drawn to some animals, particularly when they are young. Apparently, some animals elicit the same kind of parental feelings as those toward babies, thus explaining the age regression over time of cartoon characters like Mickey Mouse.

what he is in potentiality, his handiwork manifests in activity.[38]

We are willing to make sacrifices for others because we choose and love the virtuous life. Since a virtuous life is one constituted by activity, and is in a sense productive of itself, then we love the things we do according to virtue, irrespective of the utilitarian value it may generate. In other words, virtuous activity is its own reward because *it is the good life*, and a source of greater pleasure than actions aimed at personal utility. It is from this perspective that Aristotle concludes that mothers may be willing to sacrifice their personal happiness for the sake of their children's prosperity, even if their children give them nothing in return. Within this conception, we can be beneficent to the nonhuman world as an aspect of contributing to the common good, without expecting honor in return, given our desire to live in accordance with virtue, and keeping in mind that this desire is ultimately derived from the broader environment within which the good life is pursued (i.e. a good life is dependent upon a good or sustainable environment).

In a manner of speaking, we are being quite selfish by benefitting others for their sake, or by sacrificing personal well-being for the sake of the common good. As mentioned previously, virtuous human beings may engage in a kind of moral competition, each seeking to outdo others in virtuous activity. By forfeiting our wealth or sacrificing our lives for the sake of others, we are actually assigning ourselves the greater good (i.e. nobility) and denying others the opportunity to do what is noble. In many if not most instances,

[38] *Nicomachean Ethics* IX.7, 1168a5-9.

this would be mutually beneficial, although some may benefit more than others. Yet on the other hand, in times of conflict or of limited resources, circumstances may dictate that someone be a loser.

FRIENDSHIP, VIRTUE AND THE POSSIBILITY OF CONFLICT

That the world is a finite place is a fact recognized by Aristotle.[39] Thus, the possibility of conflict between individuals or groups competing for the same resource(s) may arise. This was the assumption Aristotle held in his discussion of the importance of government being founded upon principles of justice.[40] In situations in which all citizens are of equal ability, then justice demands that they take turns in governing and being governed, since all cannot govern at the same time. In some situations, if a citizen monopolizes political affairs because of his greater influence, then it may be necessary to ostracize or ban that individual from the city for some period of time for the sake of the common interest.[41] A good citizen among others of equal ability will therefore choose to both govern and be governed, with the result that he willingly sacrifices personal success for the sake of general well-being:

> Now what is right must be construed as equally right, and what is equally right is to be considered with reference to the advantage of the state, and the common good of the citizens. And a citizen is one who shares in governing and being governed. He differs under different forms of government, but in the best state

[39] Lear, 1988, 73.

[40] *Politics* VII.14, 1332b13-40.

[41] *Politics* III.13.

> he is one who is able and chooses to be governed and to govern with a view to the life of excellence.[42]

Shortages are also possible with respect to external goods, as indicated by their importance in providing the resources needed to lead a good life.[43] Such is the case for the basic necessities like food and shelter, but can also include other things like friends and personal beauty. In our relationship with friends, Aristotle says that we should be quick to share our good fortune with others, but hesitate to share our misfortune.[44] Since we are concerned with their good for their sake, we do not want to do anything that may diminish their well-being, focusing instead on doing what we can to enhance their lives. Again, Aristotle is stressing the greater importance of the common good over one's own individual good, and stating that we should be willing to endure pain for others. Consulting with our friends during periods of grief or some other bad fortune may make us feel better and help rekindle our spirit, but at the expense of our friend's prosperity. Thus, a person of good character will hesitate in being the cause of a friend's distress, but will go readily to the aid of those facing adversity.

If it is true that we both can and should express benevolent-regard toward the nonhuman world, then what does virtue dictate for human behavior in times of conflict with that world? Given that our relationship to other species is quite mixed, our motivation for

---

42 *Politics* III.13, 1283b40-1284a2.

43 *Nicomachean Ethics* I.8, 1099a32-b8 and 1101a14-16.

44 *Nicomachean Ethics* IX.11.

preserving them may also be mixed. With respect to friends, we find their continued existence to be desirable for both their instrumental and inherent value. In other words, we do not view them strictly as means to an end, or as ends in themselves. Both aspects play an inseparable part in any friendship. We have friends in part because they satisfy our need to associate with people of comparable character. They enhance our existence by providing stimulating conversation and comradery, help us during times of need, provide us with opportunities to do fine deeds, etc. But because they are our friends, we also want to enhance their lives for their sake, even if that might entail self-sacrifice. Our motive for preserving friendship is thus not strictly altruistic, nor is it strictly egoistic. Terence Irwin writes:

> Clearly the virtuous person's attitude to his friend's good is not entirely selfless and self-forgetful. But Aristotle takes it to be consistent with concern for the friend's good for his own sake. It is because this sort of concern is fine that the virtuous person thinks it is part of his good. Hence the virtuous friend never 'sacrifices himself', if that implies sacrifice of his own interest to another's; but he is no less concerned for the friend's good for the friend's own sake than a 'self-sacrificing' person would be.[45]

On this interpretation, our willingness to sacrifice our interests for the sake of nonhuman "friends", would not be nearly as great as it would be for our human friends. The primary reason is that it is our friend's understanding that we love most of all, and that which we seek to preserve. Nonhuman beings lack the ability to reason, and thus lack understanding. Therefore, they are not to be accorded the same consideration we should give our human friends of good

[45] Quoted in Annas, 1989, 11.

character. Their interests must be of secondary concern to human interests, and their value as instruments would normally predominate over their value as beings with inherent goodness. An important point, however, is that there may arise situations requiring the sacrifice of our interests for the sake of our nonhuman "friends" that emerge from the principle of self-love.

The basis for the conclusion above originates in my sense that Aristotle does not claim that the love of a friend's understanding is the only reason motivating us to act for their sake. If that were the case, then I would be at a loss to explain why he appears to think it acceptable to benefit others lacking virtue for their sake and without expecting anything in return. Such is the case with respect to children, and perhaps to our parents. Clearly children are not born with virtuous reasoning ability with respect to either practical or theoretical matters. It is something that must be nurtured through habituation and instruction over a considerable period of time, and often against their expressed will. Nor does Aristotle ever indicate in the *Nicomachean Ethics* that our parents must be of virtuous character before we need honor them. Aristotle simply says that we should honor them and are forever in their debt for giving us life.

I interpret Aristotle as saying that it is not just understanding that we love in ourselves or others, but at a more basic level, we also love the desire to understand. As human beings, our understanding is something that we should love most of all, because that is what defines us most of all. But that does not exhaust our existence. We are also composite beings of form and matter that must be continuously supplied with external goods to keep us going. Human soul is also divided into many parts, only one of which is unique among animals, and is the authoritative element in our being (i.e. the rational part). Since living according to our nature does not come about naturally, we must labor to bring about virtue in ourselves and others. When we act for the sake of children, for example, we do so because we know that they *can become* active understanders of the world, not that they already are. It is their potential to understand that is being taken into consideration when we make sacrifices for them.

Nonhuman life is not all that different. They too have a desire to understand, although it will never be satisfied within themselves. Lacking mind, they live without the ability for self-understanding, and thus cannot fully actualize their form within their own being. However, self-understanding may exist outside of themselves in a mind that is actively thinking their form. Such is always the case for God, and sometimes the case for human beings. But the desire is the same for all life, including nonhumans. They too are potential understanders, although that potential is not realizable for them in their composite existence. In a way, they are expressing their desire to understand by being understood, as they project perceptible form onto the sense faculty of a suitably placed perceiver. If that perceiver in turn has a mind that is able to become the intelligible form of the nonhuman being, then what is understanding from the perspective of the understander, is self-understanding from the perspective of the thing being understood, since thought and the object of thought are the same.[46] Therefore, if we can (or should) sacrifice our inter-

---

46 This is not to imply that the nonhuman world is somehow dependent upon humans to actualize form. My only point is that nonhuman beings, although lack-

ests for the sake of children, then I can ascertain no reason why we could not (or should not) sacrifice our interests for the sake of other beings moved by the desire to understand in an appropriate way.

Yet even if we determine that such an argument is not valid – that there is no rational basis for benefiting other living beings in terms of their potential for self-understanding, I think Aristotle's conception of self-love and friendship remains capable of expressing a moral responsibility toward the nonhuman world that may entail sacrificing our interests for their well-being. For example, if it is true that the good of the whole takes precedence over the good of the part, and therefore the good of the larger environment takes precedence over the good of any component part (including human beings), then it becomes reasonable to accept that human beings can be motivated to sacrifice personal or collective well-being, if that sustains the conditions for happiness. Such a situation might arise if human beings were to live in a way that either eroded or threatened our ability to acquire natural resources contingent for life, or diminished our ability to encounter other species contingent for the good human life. The virtuous person would be motivated to protect the integrity of the environment, because he or she knows that by doing so, he or she would be protecting the conditions for happiness or self-understanding.

Julia Annas stated that the concept of self-love is basic to Aristotle's ethics, rather than peripheral, and cannot be restricted to

---

ing self-understanding, are still driven by the same force that compels humans to actively study the world around them.

the discussion of friendship.[47] I think her conclusion is quite right, but perhaps does not go far enough. As I interpret Aristotle more broadly, I am led to believe that self-love is a fundamental component of his thinking, and not limited to his moral philosophy. Once we recognize that self-love is actually a love of understanding, then we can begin to grasp the fundamental role it plays in Aristotle's life and thought. I think we can also begin to appreciate why there is a basis in the Aristotelian tradition to be concerned for the welfare of nonhuman beings for their own sake and should be willing to do more than exhibit goodwill for the rest of the natural world - even if that means self-sacrifice either as individuals or as a species.

Today, we are currently witnessing the mass extinction of a significant percentage of the world's flora and fauna due primarily to habitat destruction that may imperil our future.[48] Although extinction is the eventual fate of all species, the current rate of extinction is estimated to be 1,000 to 10,000 times greater than the normal background rate.[49] The majority of those being extinguished are invertebrates or what may be described as ignoble creatures, perhaps explaining the relative lack of concern about their demise among most people. Yet, if Aristotle is to be believed, even they should be respected as a source of wonder and beauty, and worthy of our ef-

47 Annas, 1989, 13 & 15.

48 IPBES. 2019. Global assessment report on biodiversity and ecosystem services of the Intergovernmental Science-Policy Platform on Biodiversity and Ecosystem Services. E. S. Brondizio, J. Setttele, S. Diaz, and H. T. Ngo (editors). IPBES Secretariat, Bonn, Germany.

49 Chivian and Bernstein, *Sustaining Life: How Human Health Depends on Biodiversity*, 2008.

forts to preserve them.

CONCLUSION

In this chapter I have attempted to determine if Aristotle's moral philosophy is capable of generating a justifiable reason to benefit the nonhuman world for their sake based upon his discussion of friendship and its relationship to the concept of self-love. I have characterized the human/nonhuman relationship as involving benevolent-regard, since it is not based upon mutual affection (in the way friendship is) yet goes well beyond Aristotle's conception of goodwill. Benevolent-regard is possible because I understand Aristotle to be saying that a true self-lover is one who loves not only understanding most of all, but the desire to understand as well. Otherwise his discussion of our responsibility to children and others who lack the appropriate virtues makes little sense. If it is true that a self-lover also loves the desire to understand, and not understanding alone, then it stands to reason that we can also act for the sake of all beings that embody such a desire. I think it evident that Aristotle considered all living beings to manifest the desire to understand (defining their being) irrespective of the fact that nonhuman species are incapable of self-understanding. It is on this account that we can have a moral responsibility to act on their behalf for their own sake.

Additionally, since all life is integrated as part to whole, I also interpret Aristotle as saying that a self-lover is one who acts primarily for the benefit of the common good, including the good of the natural world taken as a whole, as expressed in terms of environmental integrity. This is a consequence of human dependency on the natural world, both for our very existence and for happiness. It is our ultimate dependency upon the rest of the natural world that provides the utilitarian foundation for environmental concern in general, and species preservation in particular. This is true because in order to live well, we must first live, and also because the richness of our understanding is directly related to the world's diversity and complexity.

Beyond any utilitarian considerations to preserve environmental integrity, the implications of Aristotle's discussion of friendship in chapters 8 and 9 of the *Nicomachean Ethics* suggests that acting on behalf of the nonhuman world for its sake can be viewed as an expression of human virtue. In other words, undertaking actions that lead to sustaining environmental integrity and the common good is a component of virtue. This is because the preservation of environmental integrity is prior to, and is an important requirement for, the well-being of society, or any individual member of society.

NOTES

Julia Annas, "Self-Love in Aristotle," *The Southern Journal of Philosophy* 27 (1989): 1-18.

Eric Chivian and Aaron Bernstein, *Sustaining Life: How Human Health Depends on Biodiversity* (New York: Oxford University Press, 2008).

E. S. Brondizio, J. Settele, S. Diez, and H.T. Ngo (eds). IPBES. "Global assessment report on biodiversity and ecosystem services of the intergovernmental science-policy platform on biodiversity and ecosystem services," (2019), IPBES Secretariat, Bonn, Germany.

Richard Kraut, *Aristotle on the Human Good* (Princeton, NJ: Princeton University Press, 1989).

Jonathan Lear, *Aristotle: The Desire to Understand* (New York: Cambridge University Press, 1988).

CHAPTER 6: EUDAIMONIA AND ENVIRONMENTAL SUSTAINABILITY

INTRODUCTION

For Aristotle, the question of the good life is one that cannot be answered in abstraction of a system of morality. This is because the ethical life and the good life are different terms for the same thing. Striving to live well, or develop into a good person as a member of a good society, is to live ethically. As discussed in Chapter 2, one purpose of the *Nicomachean Ethics* was to persuade others that living ethically is not only good in itself, but is also a prerequisite for achieving complete success or perfect happiness in life. The moral virtues by themselves may not be sufficient for realizing the best possible life, but they nevertheless can result in a good and meaningful life:

> ... for man, therefore, the life according to intellect is best and pleasantest, since intellect more than anything else is man. This life therefore is also the happiest ... But in a secondary degree the life in accordance with the other kind of excellence is happy; for the activities in accordance with this befit our human estate.[1]

Aristotle goes on to say that although the best life is defined in terms of intellectual virtue, we cannot overlook the importance of the ethical virtues, since we are both mortal and human. As he says, "...in so far as he is a man and lives with a number of people, he chooses to do excellent acts...".[2] Given our biological and mortal nature, happi-

---

1 *Nicomachean Ethics* X.7 & 8, 1178a6-10.

2 *Nicomachean Ethics* X.8, 1178b5-6.

ness must be realized from within the physical and political systems of relationship that circumscribe our existence on earth.

An important problem recognized by Aristotle is that a truly virtuous life can be difficult to attain. Few people seem able to develop the character traits that foster successful living. This difficulty in attaining virtue is often the result of not having an adequate support system to help guide potential aspirants along a virtuous path - an indispensable element, given that human nature is not expressed "naturally". This helps to explain the emphasis Aristotle places upon the common social or political good, and why it has priority over the individual. The same can be said of the larger environmental commons providing the necessary resources allowing communities and social institutions to exist. Thus, I would argue that Aristotle has an implicit (if not explicit) hierarchical structure that ultimately gives priority to environmental integrity, since we cannot even envision living well if the prerequisites for life itself are not addressed first. It is this conception of Aristotelian interdependency that should provide a fairly easy entrance into current discussions of sustainability.

However, applying an Aristotelian morality to modern times is of little consequence if it is only a matter of historical interest, with little if any resonance for us moderns, as has been argued. On my reading, however, Aristotle appears to have as much potency today as in the remote past. Many of the questions he raised, at least with respect to issues of morality, remain of vital interest today. Aristotelian scholars continue to crank out a seemingly endless stream of research and commentary on his remarkable philosophical works, not all of which is purely esoteric or an exercise in philosophical archeology. As I hope to illustrate in this chapter, the ancient Macedonian may still have something to offer us moderns as we lurch toward ecological sustainability, despite the apparent challenges posed by living an ethical life.

MORALITY AND DESIRE

An important element in Aristotle's discussion of happiness is the distinction he makes between the end product of activities, and activities that are ends themselves.[3] Bridle-making, for example, is aimed at the production of an artifact distinct from the activity producing it. According to Aristotle, it is the nature of ends to be better than the activities leading to their fabrication. In this case, bridles have greater worth than the activity of bridle-making. On the other hand, some activities are themselves ends, and are the object of interest or desire. These activities are at the core of Aristotelian ethics insofar as virtuous activity constitutes happiness. There is no artifact produced or gold star bestowed on an individual once all the virtues have been exhibited. Rather, it is the ongoing **process** of virtuous living that characterizes a successful life.

Upon my reading, Aristotle also claims that the ethical landscape is grounded in motivation as an expression of desire. It is insufficient to say that our moral beliefs urge us to behave in a certain way, since his conception of morality is derived from a motive force inherent in human nature. Which is to say that **all** human action is grounded in desire. This led Lear to conclude that the *Nicomachean Ethics* was

3 *Nicomachean Ethics* I.1.

not meant to persuade people to be good or to advise them how to behave properly in various circumstances. Rather, Lear maintained that Aristotle was offering self-understanding to people as a means to comprehend their desire to live virtuously.[4] Aristotle is, in a sense, preaching to the converted. He is giving virtuous people good reason and insight to better understand and affirm their motivation or desire to live according to virtue.

For Aristotle, to deliberate well about practical matters is an extension of our motivation to satisfy our more sophisticated desires. This is made possible because desire is a common component in all parts of human soul.[5] Practical thinking differs from theoretical thinking in that it is concerned with deliberating about means to satisfy a desire. A person of ethical virtue would then be a person able to deliberate well about choosing one course of action over another, so long as she desires nothing amiss. Deliberating well and choosing correctly among different options is characteristic of an organized soul. An ethically virtuous person knows both what should be desired and how it can be satisfied. Her soul becomes harmonious, and exhibits a clarity that is lacking in people without practical wisdom. Such a structured system of morality can only help in providing direction to one's life, and thus rendering decision-making less muddled or inconsistent.

One reason to explain why a person of good character has knowledge of what constitutes right desire is that Aristotle consid-

4 Lear, 1988, 157.

5 *On the Soul* III.9-10.

ered both ethical and theoretical virtue to be concerned with truth.[6] This is not to claim that ethical and theoretical truth have the same level of certainty associated with each. What is true scientifically, for example, cannot be otherwise and is thus amenable to precision. Practical truth, on the other hand, is not demonstrable, and necessarily lacks complete certainty. This leads him to offer the following qualification in the *Nicomachean Ethics*:

> Our discussion will be adequate if it has as much clearness as the subject-matter admits of; for precision is not to be sought for alike in all discussions, any more than in all the products of the crafts. Now fine and just actions, which political science investigates, exhibit much variety and fluctuation, so that they may be thought to exist only by convention, and not by nature. And goods also exhibit a similar fluctuation because they bring harm to many people; for before now men have been undone by reason of their wealth, and others by reason of their courage. We must be content, then, in speaking of such subjects and with such premises to indicate the truth roughly and in outline, and in speaking about things which are only for the most part true and with premises of the same kind to reach conclusions that are no better. In the same spirit, therefore, should each of our statements be *received*; for it is the mark of an educated man to look for precision in each class of things just so far as the nature of the subject admits: it is evidently equally foolish to accept probable reasoning from a mathematician and to demand from a rhetorician demonstrative proofs.[7]

The important point here is that even if we are unable to develop the same level of precision in moral matters as we can in the scientific domain, we are still obligated to achieve as much intelligibility as possible by allowing moral questions to be guided by reason.

6 *Nicomachean Ethics* VI.2.

7 1094b12-27.

Thus, our desire to act in a specific way to achieve a specific end is not the result of some urge that just happens to bubble up. Rather, it is the result of what Aristotle calls right desire, based upon a reflective understanding of the situation. This will give structure to our lives and place us in a better position to achieve coherence in both thinking and action.

THE COMMON GOOD

Given the priority Aristotle accords the greater good, a successful life can come at great cost to a person of good character. Virtue may demand, for example, that an individual sacrifice his well-being, perhaps to the extent of life itself, for the sake of the greater good. As I have attempted to argue in the previous chapters, I think this true with respect to both social and ecological communities of interaction. This conclusion is derived from my interpretation of Aristotle being neither an egoist nor an anthropocentrist. That he is not an egoist is evident in his discussion of friendship, where he states that one should benefit a friend for his own sake. Although he characterizes our regard for friends in terms of self-love, the Aristotelian "self" in this instance does not entail a love for our discrete, composite, individual beings. Rather, "self" is defined in terms of one's understanding – the ruling element of the human species, and that for the sake of which we should order our lives. This particular conception of "self" leads Aristotle to conclude that virtue dictates a willingness to suffer pain, perhaps even the pain of death, in order to attain happiness. It is ultimately the well-being of the greater good that has priority:

> For even if the end is the same for a single man and for a state, that of the state seems at all events something greater and more complete both to attain and to preserve; for though it is worthwhile to attain the end merely for one man, it is finer and more godlike to attain it for a nation or for city-states.[8]

Although Aristotle does not here mention the importance of preserving the environment, I think it would be a mistake to conclude that his ethics are incapable of generating environmental concern, and thus of not being willing to act, even to the extent of self-sacrifice, on behalf of environmental integrity.[9] Aristotle was well aware that individual or collective happiness was ultimately dependent upon the beneficence of nature. Part of his concern was derived from the self-evident acknowledgement that in order to live well, one must first live. That is why he insisted that people must be sufficiently equipped with external goods in order to pursue the good life. We must have such things as food in order to sustain our bodies and sufficient wealth to satisfy other material needs, and provide the leisure time necessary for leading an excellent life. Since these needs are satisfied and provided for by nature, it would be negligent (if not a vice) to behave in a way that would threaten the conditions of existence. In addition, only through our observation and study of the natural domain, in part and as a whole, are we able to understand the world and achieve complete happiness. The richness of our understanding, and thus the richness of human happiness, is

8 *Nicomachean Ethics* I.4, 1094b7-10.

9 I am a bit uncomfortable with labeling the effort to maintain environmental integrity to be a "sacrifice," since sacrifice in this context refers to sustaining the conditions for existence. I owe this insight to Hopper, 1991, 75.

directly related to the richness and well-being of the natural world. If this much is true, then it stands to reason that, at least in some situations, it may be necessary for human beings, either as individuals or as a community, to sacrifice immediate interests for the greater ecological good.

The possibility for sacrificing our interest for the sake of other species, or for the environment as a whole, within the Aristotelian tradition can also be supported by a perspective that does not make human beings the measure of all value. Clearly, Aristotle considers virtuous people to be superior to other perishable beings, but he does not consider human beings to be the best of all things. That honor is reserved for God who is most good and blessed. The best human life consists of becoming God-like insofar as possible. As mentioned earlier, Aristotle urges us to transcend our particular human existence to live a life that is divine - the paradigm of flourishing. If he were saying that human beings were the measure of all things, then it becomes very difficult to account for his insistence on living a life that is not strictly human. And if it is true that we should love and honor God as the source of life, then I would find it logically inconsistent to not also love and honor all life in some way that is the physical manifestation of God's understanding.

An interesting element in this discussion is that Aristotle does not leave us with a clear indication of the relative value of human existence as compared to that of other species. We can only be sure that he considered human life to be *potentially* superior to that of other composite beings. He makes no claims that all human beings, simply because they are human, are of greater worth than other animals. In fact, he clearly indicates that most people are not good, and that when people live lives contrary to virtue, they can be the worst of all animals. This judgement is brought out in both the *Nicomachean Ethics* and the *Politics*. For example, in II.9 of the *Nicomachean Ethics*, Aristotle discusses why good people are so rare:

> That moral excellence is a mean, then, and in what sense it is so, and that it is a mean between two vices, the one involving excess, the other deficiency, and that it is such because its character is to aim at what is intermediate in passions and actions, has been sufficiently stated. Hence also it is no easy task to be good. For in everything it is no easy task to find the middle, e.g. to find the middle of a circle is not for every one but for him who know; so, too, any one can get angry -- that is easy -- or give or spend money; but to do this to the right person, to the right extent, at the right time, with the right aim, and in the right way, *that* is not for every one, nor is it easy; that is why goodness is both rare and laudable and noble.[10]

It would seem that living according to the mean in all the relevant ways is far from easy. It takes effort, training, and experience - things that are often in short supply leading to the rather curious observation that human beings, unlike the other animals, must struggle to realize their nature.

By the end of the *Nicomachean Ethics*, Aristotle seems resigned to the fact that even under optimal circumstances of good training and education, most people must be compelled to obey what is noble and good:

> ...it is surely not enough that when [people] are young they should get the right nurture and attention; since they must,

---

10 1109a20-29.

> even when they are grown up, practise and be habituated to them, we shall need laws for this as well, and generally speaking to cover the whole of life; for most people obey necessity rather than argument, and punishments rather than what is noble.[11]

This leaves us with a relatively pessimistic appreciation of the capacity of people to realize their potential. If the life of virtue is an expression of human freedom, then it appears that most people are constrained by intellectual shackles. And in those situations where human beings are completely separated from law and justice, then there can be no hope for them at all, as they will become utterly corrupt:

> A social instinct is implanted in all men by nature, and yet he who first founded the state was the greatest of benefactors. For man, when perfected, is the best of animals, but, when separated from law and justice, he is the worst of all ... That is why, if he has not excellence, he is the most unholy and the most savage of animals, and the most full of lust and gluttony. But justice is the bond of men in states; for the administration of justice, which is the determination of what is just, is the principle of order in political society.[12]

If it is the case that individual men without virtue are the worst of all animals, or at least of lesser value than other species of life, then there is no basis to take the interests of all men over that of all other beings in all situations. Although I will not pursue such questions, the quote above makes clear that there is also much to be explored with respect to the expectations and responsibilities people have toward each other as part of a common good, including environ-

---

[11] 1180a1-5.

[12] *Politics* I.2, 1253a30-33, 36-40.

mental considerations, that are reflected in principles of justice.

ARISTOTLE AND CONTEMPORARY LIFE

There remains the question of the relevancy for the modern world of an Aristotelian approach to sustainability issues in general, and to environmental ethics in particular. Harlow claimed that the kind of ontological presuppositions that would make an Aristotelian worldview possible are no longer available to us.[13] This formed the basis of her criticism of Rolston's defense of nonanthropocentrism in that his arguments were similar to those of Aristotle. If I understand her correctly, Harlow is claiming that the conception of the world that maintains (1) a notion of an independent (of human reference) objective order of the good, and (2) an association of good with teleology, is dead. Harlow reasons that the modern world is constrained by a linguistic dependent view of nature. In other words, the natural world that we encounter in everyday experience is constituted by cognitive and linguistic activity, and is thus a cultural product. We cannot return to an Aristotelian conception of nature in large part because modern thought embodies a different paradigm that is unable to coexist (at least not comfortably) with the older teleological paradigm.

While it is certainly true that the western world has undergone dramatic cultural changes since the reign of the ancient Greeks, and thus it can be claimed that we live in very different worlds, I think the Aristotelian tradition still has resonance for modern life – includ-

13 Harlow, *The Human Face of Nature*, 1992.

ing modern environmentalism. This is made most clear in relation to Aristotle's recognition that human life exists in an interdependent world. Although his primary concern was to illuminate the social interdependency of humans, as I have argued throughout this work, he was quite aware of the interdependency of life - including human life - as lived in nature. As it was for the ancient Greeks, we are fundamentally dependent upon the natural world for our well-being, and that dependency shapes how we live our lives on Earth. Culture and language may have changed dramatically over the intervening 2500 or so years, but not our reliance upon natural resources.

It is also worth noting the ongoing and earnest contemporary philosophical discussion of, and support for, the resurrection of the Aristotelian tradition in some form or another in the modern era. For example, Alisdair MacIntyre said the following:

> It is...the case that the crucial moral opposition is between liberal individualism in some version or other and the Aristotelian tradition in some version or other. The differences between the two run very deep. They extend beyond ethics and morality to the understanding of human action, so that rival conceptions of the social sciences, of their limits and their possibilities are intimately bound up with the antagonistic confrontation of these two alternative ways of viewing the human world...My own conclusion is very clear. It is that on the one hand we still, in spite of the efforts of three centuries of moral philosophy and one of sociology, lack any coherent rationally defensible statement of a liberal individualist point of view; and that, on the other hand, the Aristotelian tradition can be restated in a way that restores intelligibility and rationality to our moral and social attitudes and commitments.[14]

14 MacIntyre, *After Virtue.* 2007, 259.

Regarding the publication of his book *Retrieving Aristotle in an Age of Crisis*, David Roochnik said more recently:

> It argues that even today, in fact especially today, mired as we are in a crisis of our own making...it is both possible and reasonable to prefer Aristotle's world. ...Aristotle gives a rational account, a theory, of the world from top to bottom and it does much: it teaches us about the world to which *we* actually live.[15]

Modern defenses of the Aristotelian tradition (irrespective of motivation) are not an attempt to recapture a long-forgotten or neglected area of scholarship. As noted by Barnes, reflection on Aristotle's philosophy has never really stopped:

> ...Aristotle's writings have been subjected, ever since antiquity, to profound and continuous critical attention. Learned articles and learned books, scholarly commentaries and popular accounts, philological inquiries and philosophical investigations, the colloquia and symposia - scribble, scribble, scribble, for two thousand years, and never faster than in recent decades No waste paper basket can keep up with the stuff.[16]

All this intellectual activity is hardly indicative of a philosophical dead end.

I should also note that while some of the earlier environmental philosophers questioned the desirability or even feasibility of an Aristotelian approach to the ethics of environmental concern, more recent voices have offered an alternative perspective. Bhuiyan,[17] for

---

15 Roochnik, *Retrieving Aristotle in an Age of Crisis*, 2013, xiv.

16 Barnes, *The Cambridge Companion to Aristotle*, 1995, xii.

17 Bhuiyan, *Is Aristotle's Philosophy Anthropocentric?*, 2015.

example, argues that Aristotle's teleology is actually biocentric. This conclusion emerges from the recognition that, within Aristotelian metaphysics, all life consists of both form and matter - thus all living things have a "purposeful directed life" as an expression of soul. Oele[18] seeks to reassess Aristotle's conception of *physis*[19] as a potential justification for assisting the natural world, currently in a state of dysfunction resulting from environmentally destructive human activity, so as to help restore nature as part of a social-ecological system. As she states:

> The *physis* that we seek to invoke is thereby not pristine, unified; it is not *other* than society or technology. Rather, the *physis* to be sought is the result of collaboration, not outside anthropomorphism but also not solely anthropocentric.[20]

Perhaps scholars like Oele represent the beginning of a period when environmental philosophers take notice of the potential efficacy of Aristotelian ideas beyond that found in virtue ethics, leading to yet more scribbling about Aristotle's writing. We shall see.

CONCLUSION

As I discussed in the first chapter, the limited appreciation of the Aristotelian tradition within the relatively new discipline of environmental philosophy may be due to the perception among some of its early scholars that ancient Greek philosophy in general, and perhaps

18 Oele, *Folding Nature Back Upon Itself*, 2017.

19 *Physis* is most commonly translated as "nature" in the sense of a living being having a "nature."

20 Oele, 2017, 10.

Aristotelianism in particular, has contributed a metaphysical system at odds with environmental protection. It has been my purpose in this book to counter that perception by demonstrating the potential relevance of the Aristotelian tradition for contemplating the critically important environmental challenges that we currently face. As reflected in the comment by Roochnik above, Aristotle makes clear that a good or successful life cannot be realized in abstraction of either the social or ecological conditions of existence. His philosophy seems quite capable of offering a substantive way to engage in the modern challenge of ecological sustainability. In fact, my sense is that efforts aimed at the preservation of environmental integrity are obligatory within the Aristotelian tradition, since complete human happiness or success is absolutely dependent upon a sustainable and diverse environment. There is thus to be found in Aristotle's moral philosophy not only a basis for environmental concern, but an implicit moral foundation for *action* on behalf of environmental integrity. In other words, it is not enough simply to care about a sustainable world, one must actually **do** something to ensure the realization of a sustainable lifestyle.

Of course, framing the goal of human development within an Aristotelian conception of *eudaimonia*, or happiness, may be asking too much. Can we meaningfully assert that the best life for human beings is one lived in accordance with intellectual virtue, even if we leave aside the fundamental role played by an unmoved mover? Aristotle actually provides a means to address this kind of question that may be helpful. According to Lear,[21] in preparing the *Nicomachean Ethics*, Aristotle did not try to convince everyone that the good life is as he describes it. Rather, he was simply trying to provide a reflective endorsement to those already living a life devoted to virtuous activity, that their lives were indeed good. We may not be able to state with certainty that the life of intellectual virtue is best, but if people were to pattern their lives in a way that at least approximated the Aristotelian ideal, then I think it would be difficult to say that human life on Earth had no merit. Perhaps this is all we can ask of any ethic that purports to express the nature of living well in a world of limits. The Aristotelian tradition at least provides a vision for living that is ecologically sound. The challenge for practical Aristotelian scholars is to define that vision in terms applicable to contemporary life.

NOTES

Jonathan Barnes, *The Cambridge Companion to Aristotle* (New York: Cambridge University Press, 1995).

A.S.M. Anwarullah Bhuiyan, "Is Aristotle's Philosophy Anthropocentric? A Biocentric Defense of the Aristotelian Philosophy of Nature," *Biocosmology-Neo-Aristotelism* 5 (2) (2015).

---

[21] Lear, 1988, section 5.1.

Elizabeth M. Harlow, "The Human Face of Nature: Environmental Values and the Limits of Nonanthropocentrism," *Environmental Ethics* 14 (1)(1992): 27-42.

David H. Hopper, *Technology, Theology, and the Idea of Progress* (Louisville, KY: John Knox Press, 1991).

Jonathan Lear, *Aristotle: The Desire to Understand* (New York: Cambridge University Press, 1988).

Alasdair MacIntyre, *After Virtue,* 3rd (Notre Dame: University of Notre Dame Press, 2007).

Marjolein Oele, "Folding Nature Back Upon Itself: Aristotle and the Rebirth of 'Physis.'" *Philosophy* 58.

David Roochnik, *Retrieving Aristotle in an Age of Crisis* (Albany: State University of New York Press, 2013).

CHAPTER 7: MORAL PHILOSOPHY AND ENVIRONMENTAL SCIENCE

INTRODUCTION

As stated in the introduction, my motivation for digging into the philosophical details of Aristotle was rooted in an effort to answer the question of "why care about environmental protection?" This included ancillary questions like what are the outlines of sustainability as a moral concept, and how can our efforts aimed at realizing a sustainable lifestyle be justified? Having said that, while this book can reasonably be described as an exercise in environmental philosophy (and hopefully makes a positive contribution to Aristotelian scholarship), I much prefer to characterize it as an effort to explore the moral dimension of environmental problem-solving within the framework of environmental science. This is principally because I take seriously the idea that environmental science is both interdisciplinary and value-laden. It arose for the sake of addressing various environmental problems that became evident during the post-*Silent Spring* era. The desire to address environmental problems evolved with the perception that something of value was being lost, or was at risk of being lost. In a very real sense, environmental scientists have been trying to save the world from environmental destruction, and ideally to chart a course toward an ecologically sustainable society. Thus, it is necessarily shaped by a sense of moral purpose. And yet little has been done within the domain of environmental science itself to explore and/or understand the values shaping the discipline or environmental problems themselves.[1] In fact, academic programs in environmental science may actually be distancing themselves from "the humanities". This is not an argument favoring the transformation of environmental science into a branch of philosophy, but of encouraging a reasonable measure of philosophical analysis as part of what it is to "do" environmental science.

Moral questions within environmental science can be examined from at least two perspectives. First is the importance of cultural values in shaping attitudes toward the environment. This has been reflected in the seminal works of White, Merchant and Hargrove as discussed in chapter 1. The second perspective incorporates our attempt to define a sustainable lifestyle. This prompts the question of what exactly constitutes a sustainable society, or a good life generally? The first perspective allows us to understand better how we came to be facing such serious challenges. The second provides guidance with respect to our choices for the future. Within the parlance of environmental science, these perspectives help us in regards to problem definition and mitigation. In what follows, I aim to examine these perspectives in greater detail within the paradigm of sustainable development, and explain why I think such concepts need to be incorporated within environmental science curricula.

---

1 Up until now I have been using the term "environmental science" in a generic sense to represent various applied environmental disciplines such as environmental studies and sustainability science. In this chapter, I am referring to the specific discipline of environmental science, although the same criticism may also apply to related disciplines.

ENVIRONMENTAL VALUES

Commentators such as Engel, Hargrove and Hughes have claimed that an important basis for modern environmental devastation has been the failure of the major moral traditions to either recognize or take seriously the ethical significance of environmental problems.[2] Hargrove sought to explain this oversight by pointing to a deep-seated skepticism of the reality of the natural world among those steeped in the western philosophical tradition. Clearly, generating environmental concern among folks not willing or able to acknowledge empirical reality constitutes a daunting challenge, to put it mildly. If true, then it becomes easier to appreciate why environmentalism or environmentalist tendencies have been relatively slow to develop and be sustained in much of the western world.

Analysis of the ontogeny of environmental problems has not been limited to discussions of philosophical malfeasance however. As discussed in chapter 1, White[3] pointed an accusing finger at the Judeo-Christian tradition and its emphasis on establishing dominion over the Earth. Merchant,[4] in an examination of the relationship between the scientific revolution and current attitudes toward the environment, argued that modern science substituted an organic worldview with one that was mechanical. Whereas western society prior to the scientific revolution shared a general belief that the cosmos was alive (from which emerged the term "Mother Earth"),

2 Engel, *Ethics of Sustainable Development,* 1991, Hargrove, 1989, and Hughes, 1975.

3 White, 1967.

4 Merchant, 1980.

it subsequently came to adopt the view that the cosmos and the earth were actually inert and lifeless. The point is that whatever is ultimately judged to be the root of our environmental problems, it is clear that worldviews shape our attitudes toward nature, and are an important component in any assessment of sustainability.

I think it true that metaphysical assumptions as embodied by worldviews are fundamentally important in giving structure to value systems within any given social community. Value systems in turn result in characteristic behaviors that can either enhance or hinder environmental protection, or more basically the kinds of attitudes that make possible the preservation or consumption of the natural world. In other words, how people come to understand the world and their place in it impacts the kind of values that are shared or expressed. These values in turn are made explicit in the kinds of behaviors that are deemed to be acceptable or unacceptable. As a consequence, those in the environmental problem-solving community (e.g. environmental and sustainability science) should try to identify and understand those values. At the very least, this process can help researchers delimit possible responses to a given problem. This is to say that ethical analysis has a niche in the toolkit of an environmental scientist, and should be reflected in environmental science curricula.

One of the challenges of value identification and analysis is that value often lies in the interstices of discussion and action. We know that laws and policies are based upon a system of values, but may be hard pressed to identify them. We also know that societies are guided by moral principles, but the average citizen often finds them difficult to define clearly. As individuals, we recognize that specific actions are "right" or "wrong", but can struggle in our efforts to articulate our perception in a systematic way. The end result is that those who care about the natural world, and want to see it protected from abuse, are not always able to offer coherent reasons why they care (or should care), or what actions must be taken. Not only can this make it difficult to identify any robust moral response to particular problems, it can also result in a group or groups of people holding potentially conflicting values relative to a problem - complicating the problem-solving process.

Values that manage to percolate to the surface of public discourse, perhaps especially as they relate to environmental issues, are frequently expressed in economic terms. This is certainly true for ecosystems like wetlands, and may represent our best strategy to ensure that protection efforts are realized through substantive policy (Dybas, 2006). The practical implication of economic valuation is that it validates our dependency upon the habitually externalized goods and services provided by nature. Economic tools have been important not only for the determination of value, but also for environmental policy development. This can be illustrated by attempts to establish a full-cost accounting model for economic activities having hidden negative costs and externalities affecting environmental quality. The purpose of this model is to provide an honest assessment of the costs and benefits of a given economic activity, in order to make more informed policy choices and to avoid, as much as possible, the negative environmental impacts of that activity. For example, if we were to include all of the environmental and healthcare costs correlated with burning gasoline into the price of a gallon of gas, the pump price would be significantly higher than what motorists currently pay.

Internalizing externalized costs would provide a clear economic signal to consume less gasoline, and foster a variety of possible responses ranging from changes in personal behavior (e.g. driving less) to stimulating technological development (e.g. alternative fuel vehicles) in order to find more affordable, sustainable, and perhaps more equitable transportation options. I think it fair to claim that by allowing the externalization of costs of fossil fuel combustion onto the commons, we have not only slowed the transition to renewable energy sources, but also unfairly impacted the common good, especially members of society not participating in the fossil fuel market. Looking forward, making clear the moral questions or foundations of the policy process (which are also effectively externalized from policy deliberation) places us in a better position to assess the relative merits of competing policy proposals by providing rational choices among articulated goals.

Values clearly give shape to the goals and objectives inherent in policy and its development, despite being obscured by a generally positivist process. Recognizing this fact will help us to understand how or why environmental policy emerges in the way it does. Moyers, for example, discussed the ideological forces shaping policy in the United States within the George W. Bush administration.[5] The title of his article, *Welcome to Doomsday*, reflected both his percep-

---

[5] Moyers, *Welcome to Doomsday*, 2005.

tion of how things were going and the evangelical worldview that may have contributed ideological grist to the Bush environmental policy mill. If the apocalyptic moral vision described by Moyers was not providing the kind of guidance needed to successfully identify a path to sustainability, then what were (are) the alternatives? Addressing this kind of question may be more difficult than it was during the second Bush presidency, as we enter the so-called "post truth" political environment with its apparent empirical relativism – but that does not mean the task is impossible or should be avoided. In fact, I would argue that, despite the challenges, developing a clear moral justification for ordering social political/economic structures compatible with a sustainable form of development is becoming ever more critical, given the serious and increasingly global problems we face collectively.

Scientific investigations can also be relevant to discussions of value. One can argue that the primary reason we have become so concerned about the long-term viability of ecosystems like wetlands, is that we now better understand the services they provide as part of an integrated social/ecological system. Consequently, managing for environmental sustainability has become a moral issue. This is not to say that the so-called is/ought dichotomy is being transgressed, but that facts can inform moral decision-making. Stating the fact that the ingestion of lead is hazardous to human health, particularly to children, does not constitute a moral prescription. Yet if health and children are important to us, then we ought to eliminate the hazard, lest we fail in our moral duty. To the extent that our environment contributes to human well-being or environmental health, an obligation to engage conservation/protection efforts becomes evident.

Environmental ethics can be seen as a response to the failure of modern value systems to adequately account for the moral significance of the environment. Perhaps it would be more accurate to say that environmental ethics is a response to the dominant worldview, given that various environmentally sensitive alternatives have been and continue to be expressed over time. Sustainable development, conceived as a social paradigm of practical activity situated within ecological processes, has in turn been defined as a reaction to the perceived failure of the dominant paradigm of economic development. The two are related in that the mode of development represents an overt manifestation of values drawn from a particular worldview, and upholding a conception of the human good toward which development aims. This led Engel to conclude that the moral content of sustainable development must be examined in all its detail before we can begin to pursue rationally the goal of development (i.e. ends and means are not independent variables).

If it is true that sustainable development represents a global ethic, then it is critical that we explore the nature of this still-evolving moral program, especially considering its practical significance. The paradigm of sustainable development is, after all, expressing a desire to go well beyond statements of faith or the setting down of moral principles. It is after *action*, or ways of realizing a higher quality of life without compromising ecological sustainability. In so doing, it also transcends the traditional post-World War II emphasis on stimulating economic growth as a means to fulfill other dimensions of human well-being. This more inclusive perspective was reflected in a statement by UNESCO when the idea of sustainable development was first being defined as an emerging paradigm:

> [Economic growth] provides the means of producing the goods and services that are essential for material well-being, but development, in order to fulfil material as well as spiritual aspirations and further the development of the creative capacities of each individual, should encompass all aspects of life. Furthermore, the ethical concept of equality constitutes an essential factor in development, in relation to which it should be possible to conduct and assess economic growth ... It would appear that the real challenge is not so much to get back to the rhythm and pattern of growth that, far from being confined to the economic field alone, includes objectives of cultural and human development and makes it possible to satisfy the overall needs and aspirations of humanity.[6]

One question arising from the above is how are we to determine human needs and aspirations? Put another way, what is the goal toward which development is or should be aimed?

DEFINING SUSTAINABLE DEVELOPMENT

In one of the earliest expositions addressing the ethics of sustainable development, Engel[7] listed five reasons (which remain relevant today) explaining why people should be interested in such moral questions. The first was a budding awareness of the role values play in shaping human behavior. Whereas social scientists have emphasized a value-neutral approach in the past by focusing on socio-political and economic factors in explaining human activity, it has come at the cost of excluding cultural beliefs/values forming the

6 UNESCO, *Goals of Development. 1988*, preface.

7 Engel, 1991.

core of social and economic institutions. If it is true that that social, political, and economic systems emerge from, and are bounded by, a given worldview or moral tradition, then the attempt to define development in terms of value neutrality must be considered intellectually suspect. It also suggests that nuances to development due to cultural differences may be overlooked, thus putting at risk the effectiveness of regionally focused development initiatives.

The second reason for being concerned about the ethics of sustainable development is the role morality plays in motivating people to care for the world around them, even if that means sacrificing their self-interest. This in turn may provide motivation for the third reason offered by Engel: clarifying the values implicit in policy decisions and of giving morally informed reasons to choose among alternative courses of action. The argument here is that sound and clearly articulated moral reasoning is likely to possess significantly greater practical weight than a purely positivist approach. An element of this practicality is an increased ability to persuade the public of the legitimacy of a given course of action by appealing to a shared (and defensible) set of values. If an advocate subjects their own moral viewpoint to rigorous analysis, then they will be less apt to generate vague moral concepts or policy statements that are inconsistent, incoherent, or culturally problematic.

Fourth, Engel claimed that ethics can be effective in the resolution of value conflicts among differing environmental stakeholders. This may be a particularly important element, given the relative obscurity of moral reflection and analysis in policy development – a situation that may increase the likelihood of generating initiatives that are ethically inconsistent. A conflict Engel identified in need of resolution was the ideological friction existing among preservationists and conservationists within the environmental movement. Although both are utilitarian, and define the good in terms of human welfare, they do so in quite distinct ways. Conservationism, as it came to be defined by Gifford Pinchot, was very much about the judicious use of natural resources as a means to realize economic development. The value of nature thus came to be expressed in terms of an economic resource. As Pinchot said:

> The first great fact about conservation is that it stands for development. There has been a fundamental misconception that conservation means nothing but the husbanding of resources for future generations. There could be no more serious mistake. Conservation does mean provision for the future, but it means also and first of all the recognition of the right of the present generation to the fullest necessary use of all the resources with which this country is so abundantly blessed. Conservation demands the welfare of this generation first, and afterward the welfare of the generations to follow.[8]

Preservationism, on the other hand, often emphasized the transcendental value of nature, and the importance of experiencing the natural world as a means to realize spiritual growth. John Muir, the individual most closely identified with the preservationist wing of the environmental movement, offered the following:

> The making of gardens and parks goes on with civilization all over the world, and they increase both in size and number as their value is recognized. Everybody needs beauty as well as

[8] Pinchot, *Principles of Conservation*, 1910, chapter 4: 43. I think it worthwhile to note that Pinchot devotes an entire chapter (chapter 7: *The Moral Issue*) defending conservation as a moral concept.

> bread, places to play in and pray in, where Nature may heal and cheer and give strength to body and soul alike. This natural beauty-hunger is made manifest in the little window-sill gardens of the poor, though perhaps only a geranium slip in a broken cup, as well as in the carefully tended rose and lily gardens of the rich, the thousands of spacious city parks and botanical gardens, and in our magnificent National parks--the Yellowstone, Yosemite, Sequoia, etc. -- Nature's sublime wonderlands, the admiration and joy of the world.[9]

The divergent values expressed by these two positions is perhaps best reflected in the government agencies that emerged from the efforts of each man. Whereas Pinchot was the motive force leading to the creation of the United States Forest Service (within the Department of Agriculture), Muir was the catalyst for the establishment of the United States National Park Service (within the Department of Interior). Thus, a conservationist may cast their gaze upon a forest and see a quantity of timber useful for the building of prosperous homes, while a preservationist may see instead a spiritual refuge from the dehumanizing forces of modern civilization. Both define the value of a forest in terms of human welfare, but in manifestly different ways. The differing expressions of human welfare maintained by each eventually lead to Pinchot and Muir becoming antagonists, especially with respect to the damming of the Hetch Hetchy valley in California.

The preservation/conservation division represents one manifestation of the variety of positions that have come to define the environmental movement. Sociologist Robert Brulle, for example, has identified eleven different waves or "discursive frames" of envi-

---

9 Muir, *Hetch Hetchy Valley*, 1912, chapter 16.

ronmentalism in the United States.[10] In more or less historical order they are:

> **Wildlife Management**: Wildlife should be managed to insure adequate supply to provide for the recreational use of humans in terms of hunting or fishing.
>
> **Conservation:** Natural resources should be technically managed from a utilitarian perspective to realize the greatest good for the greatest number of people over the longest period of time.
>
> **Preservation:** Nature is an important component in supporting both the physical and spiritual life of humans. Hence the continued existence of wilderness and wildlife, undisturbed by human action is necessary.
>
> **Reform Environmentalism:** Human health is linked to ecosystem conditions. To maintain a healthy human society, ecologically responsible actions are necessary. These actions can be developed and implemented through the use of natural sciences.
>
> **Environmental Health:** Human health is the outcome of interactions with physical, chemical, biological and social factors in the natural environment, especially toxic substances and pollution. To ensure community health requires a livable and healthy community, with adequate social services, and elimination of exposures to toxic or polluting substances
>
> **Deep Ecology:** The richness and diversity of all life on earth has intrinsic value, and so human life is privileged only to the extent of satisfying vital needs. Maintenance the diversity of life on earth mandates a decrease in human impacts on the natural environment, and substantial increases in the wilderness areas of the globe.
>
> **Environmental Justice:** Ecological problems occur because of the structure of society and the imperatives this structure creates for the continued exploitation of nature. Hence, the resolution of

10 Brulle, *Politics and the Environment*, 2010.

environmental problems requires fundamental social change.

EcoFeminism: Ecosystem abuse is rooted in androcentric concepts & institutions. Relations of complementarity rather than superiority between culture/nature, human/nonhuman, and male/female are needed to resolve the conflict between the human and natural worlds.

EcoSpiritualism: Nature is God's creation, and humanity has a moral obligation to keep and tend the Creation. Hence, natural and unpolluted ecosystems and biodiversity need to be preserved.

Green: All humans and their communities deserve to live in an equitable, just and environmentally sound world. Global abuses such as ecological destruction, poverty, war, and oppression are linked to global capitalism and the political and economic forces that have allowed the development of social inequality and injustices.

Animal Rights: All species have intrinsic rights to realize their own evolved characteristics, and to live an independent life free from human direction or intervention.

I don't necessarily agree with the choice of all elements for this list, or how they are characterized, but it does provide insight into the diversity of value structures (or discourses, to use Brulle's term) that have emerged in response to environmental problems that frequently will lead environmentalists in different, and perhaps conflicting, directions.[11]

---

[11] With respect to Animal Rights, Brulle characterizes it as being motivated to protect the intrinsic rights of **all** species. It would be more accurate to say they are motivated to protect the rights of individual members of **some** species having qualities deemed to be inherently valuable such as self-awareness (a quality not shared by all species or even all members within a species). He also excludes Animal Liberation, perhaps the more influential of the two animal welfare movements, and its utilitarian emphasis upon sentience, or the capacity to experience pleasure/pain (again, not co-extensive with all species or members therein). I

Most of the sub-movements within environmentalism identified by Brulle are relatively minor actors. The big three (Conservation, Preservation, Reform Environmentalism) place a strong emphasis on the instrumentality of the natural world for human welfare, and thus offer an opportunity to find common moral ground. But as indicated in the list above, not all elements of the environmental movement are derived from human utility. Deep Ecology and Animal Rights refer to intrinsic values and intrinsic rights respectively. In fact, intrinsic value has served as the foundation for many arguments justifying environmental protection. I think it true, for example, that much of the rationalization for national parks was derived from a conception of their intrinsic aesthetic appeal. While they may not have been deemed economically valuable (i.e. they made lousy farmland), they had incalculable value with respect to their beauty. Being relatively young, America lacked the great monuments of civilization such as Chartres and St. Peters Basilica in Europe. Yet, there existed natural monuments holding great cultural value for the nation (e.g. Yosemite and the Grand Canyon) that were deemed to be equally beautiful and worth preserving.

References to the aesthetic value of nature have been common since the nineteenth century in North America. Much of the content of Leopold's writings, for example, conveys his aesthetic appreciation of nature. The so-called summary moral maxim of his land ethic

---

set aside the question of the appropriateness of listing animal rights as being a variant of the environmental movement. This controversy has existed since at least 1984 with the publication of *Animal Liberation and Environmental Ethics: Bad Marriage, Quick Divorce*, by Mark Sagoff. I don't know that the dust has yet settled on this debate.

even includes the maintenance of natural beauty as an ingredient in a moral life. As he says in *The Land Ethic*, "A thing is right if it tends toward the integrity, stability and **beauty** of the biotic community. It is wrong if it tends otherwise"[12] (emphasis mine). For Leopold, even hunting was viewed as an aesthetic exercise. In the essay *Goose Music*, he relates the following:

> Poets sing and hunters scale the mountains primarily for one and the same reason - the thrill to beauty.[13]

Leopold also expressed the intrinsic value of the natural world in terms of social welfare. From another portion of the essay *Goose Music* is found the following:

> ...we have not yet learned to express the value of wildlife in terms of social welfare. Some have attempted to justify wildlife conservation in terms of meat, others in terms of personal pleasure, others in terms of cash, still others in the interest of science, education, agriculture, art, public health, and even military preparedness. But few have so far clearly realized and expressed the whole truth, namely, that all these things are but factors in a broad social value, and that wildlife...is a social asset.[14]

By "social asset," Leopold is referring to the value had from the kinds of experience that are difficult or impossible to quantify. Like Muir, Leopold argued that the direct experience of nature filled a primal human need. In addition, and similar to Aristotle, Leopold's land ethic is not philosophically abstract. In other words, it is not sufficient

---

[12] Leopold, 1966, 262.

[13] *Goose Music* in Leopold, 1966.

[14] Ibid.

to ponder goodness and beauty – one must experience it through an active engagement with the natural world. Intrinsic value of the sort described here then, is a value defined in terms of relationship.

A key contribution made by Leopold to moral philosophy was the incorporation of an ecological worldview as expressed in *The Land Ethic.* He came to argue that if we live in an ecologically interdependent world (as ecological theory asserts), then all species have a niche or role to play in the community of life, and are therefore good in some way. Thus, *The Land Ethic* not only articulates a holistic moral theory emphasizing the good of the community (or species) over that of the individual, but also challenges us to re-evaluate the value of species, perhaps especially those that have historically been reviled. The latter was most famously expressed in his essay *Thinking Like a Mountain* in which Leopold argues for the protection of wolves. As he says:

> The cowman who cleans his range of wolves does not realize that he is taking over the wolf's job of trimming the herd to fit the range. He has not learned to think like a mountain. Hence we have dustbowls, and rivers washing the future into the sea.[15]

As suggested here, one of our limitations as environmental managers has been a lack of understanding of ecological systems, and the important role played by top level predators (like wolves) in maintaining the stability and overall diversity of ecosystems. Wolves may be fearsome, potentially dangerous, and an economic threat to ranchers, but the world would be much less stable and good in

---

15 *Thinking Like a Mountain* in Leopold, 1966.

their absence. At base, *The Land Ethic* argues that our moral responsibilities must be ecologically informed and perhaps be extended beyond the boundaries of humanity.

I believe it useful to also recognize the role played by inherent value within the environmental movement. In fact, I would characterize the values expressed within Deep Ecology and Animal Rights as being inherent rather than intrinsic. The distinction is important, although the terms are frequently interchanged and can be a source of confusion. I think intrinsic value is best understood as a non-economic or qualitative value external to the object being valued. Inherent value, on the other hand, refers to a value internal to the object being valued. We can say, for example, that a work of art contains an intrinsic value not captured by its monetary worth. In fact, we may conclude that the object is so rare and unique that its value cannot be adequately captured in monetary terms (i.e. it is "priceless"). Ultimately, however, the value is not an attribute of the object in and of itself. Rather, the object reflects the value brought to it by a "valuer". Consequently, if there were no one to value the object, then it would no longer retain any value because the source of value (a "valuer") is missing. In contrast, inherent value is an internal and resident element of the object itself. Thus, if no one were present to appreciate the object, it would still be valuable because the identified value is an essential part of its being. In other words, intrinsic value is a human value that we project onto an object that is reflected back at us like light upon a mirror. An object with inherent value is itself the source of light. We perceive value that emanates from the object, not reflected from it.

The attractiveness of inherent value among some environmentalists has at least two components. First, it provides a moral justification that is not ultimately anthropocentric. When environmental ethics first distinguished itself as an identifiable field within philosophy, it did so in part by posing a challenge to anthropocentrism.[16] One question raised by this challenge was what exactly makes human beings superior to other life forms on earth? If we cannot find a rational justification for this question, then an anthropocentric value system becomes arbitrary. In addition, our inability or unwillingness to acknowledge the value of other forms of life may have caused us to devalue that life – contributing to our current environmental problems. Second, inherent value necessarily generates a prima facie duty among moral agents to respect, protect or otherwise not harm any entity possessing such value. It is therefore considered (if such an account can be defended) to be a much stronger or compelling argument than one based on instrumental, or even intrinsic, criteria. This is one reason why I developed the argument found in chapter 5. It provides an example of a potentially defensible inherent value moral argument, while also illustrating the flexibility of an Aristotelian approach to the ethics of environmental concern.

To sum up the fourth reason for pursuing an ethics of sustainability: while it may be impossible to reconcile all the potential value conflicts that exist among environmental stakeholders, if we are able to identify, clarify, or at least become cognizant of the value assumptions shaping policy, we should be better able to under-

---

16 Brennan and Lo, *Environmental Ethics*, 2016.

stand the motivations and perspectives of those stakeholders. If that much is true, then the effort to find common ground, or developing a non-arbitrary and defensible decision-making process, becomes more feasible.

The fifth and final reason that Engel mentions for having an interest in ethics is that it can contribute to the definition of a new social paradigm promoting sustainable development that is culturally appropriate. What is being questioned is not any particular part of the development process, but the entire concept of development itself as a global social paradigm. Engel argues that what we need is a new worldview as expressed in another mode of development that can provide a fulfilling and sustainable way of life for **all** human beings. Of fundamental concern to any conception of sustainable development is to define the goal of development activity that directly addresses the needs of a population. Economic growth, for example, is not the optimal target since it is an indirect measure of human welfare that does not necessarily translate into a better quality of life for most people.

ETHICS ACROSS THE ENVIRONMENTAL SCIENCE CURRICULUM

The preceding discussion is a long-winded way of stating the importance of value identification and clarification in policy, planning, and environmental problem-solving as part of efforts to realize a sustainable lifestyle. Given that the environmental sciences are ultimately concerned with identifying a path to ecological sustainability, then it stands to reason that a measure of value analysis ought to be an important component within their curricula. And yet, among the applied environmental disciplines, I have found that only conservation biology consciously and explicitly recognizes the importance of morality as a guide to action. Since its formation, conservation biologists have claimed that the loss of biodiversity is as much a moral problem as it is an ecological one. They do not study the loss of biological diversity as an intellectual exercise to satisfy their curiosity, but to learn how to redress that loss emerging from a sense of moral responsibility. This can be illustrated by the five ethical principles of conservation biology identified by Primack in a well-known textbook in the field:[17]

1. The diversity of species and biological communities should be preserved.
2. The ultimate extinction of populations and species should be prevented.
3. Ecological complexity should be maintained.
4. Evolution should continue.
5. Biological diversity has intrinsic value.

Not only do conservation biologists make explicit reference to a disciplinary moral code (not merely a professional code of conduct among members), they also embrace the proposition that the non-human world is a source of intrinsic (inherent in my definition) value - a remarkable declaration for a scientific society.

I am not personally aware of a similar statement within envi-

[17] Primack, *Essentials of Conservation Biology*, 2010, 10-11.

ronmental science, despite it having emerged at about the same time as conservation biology and for much the same reason. Even if environmental science has yet to offer an explicit ethical statement framing its disciplinary task, it would be difficult to argue that moral principles have no role to play. It seems evident that to be an environmental scientist, one must minimally be aware of the value questions that necessarily arise as part of environmental problem-solving. Why else are we engaged in environmental protection, if we do not perceive an important value there? In addition, it would be beneficial to have some familiarity with the socio-cultural context within which problem-solving occurs. All the scientific knowledge in the world is of little consequence unless it can be realized in the messy world of policy formation and application as guided by values - whether explicitly stated or not.

Historically, environmental science emerged as intellectual manifestation of the environmental movement and the perceived threats of environmental deterioration. While there is a fundamentally important scientific core in the various environmental problem-solving disciplines, their justification is rooted in the pluralist values expressed in environmentalism. These values range from inherent to instrumental, and cover a broad swath of issues, from the loss of wilderness and wildlife to the public health concerns associated with various forms of pollution (this diversity being illustrated by the "discourses" discussed by Brulle). In addition, if it is true that environmental problems can be traced to socio-cultural processes and ideologies, then the failure to investigate or acknowledge those processes and ideologies may constitute a form of malfeasance among environmental problem-solving disciplines.

Based upon personal anecdotal experience, it is my sense that practitioners of environmental science have separated themselves into distinct camps relative to their perceived social function. One camp consists of researchers defining their purpose in terms of public service on behalf of the common good. They view their professional role as involving an effort not only to understand the causes of environmental problems, but to provide solutions as well - which may entail some level of advocacy. This is consistent with the discipline having emerged in response to the modern environmental movement. In the other camp are those who see the function of environmental science as being strictly scientific, and essentially value-free - practitioners exist to help society understand environmental problems, but not step outside the boundaries of scientific objectivity to formulate or advocate a response to those problems. I think this element expresses the fear (of applied fields generally?) that the scientific legitimacy of environmental science may be compromised by defining a disciplinary purpose beyond scientific theory development.

While scientific objectivity is vital to the research process, it need not be sacrificed for the sake of seeking solutions within a socio-cultural context.[18] In addition, given that environmental problems (and their solutions) have a clear ideological component within cultural traditions, then the failure to address, acknowledge, or reflect upon those values makes little sense to me. Let us not forget that sustain-

[18] For example, see Schrader-Frechette, *Throwing out the Bathwater of Positivism, Keeping the Baby of Objectivity*, 1996.

ability is also a moral concept. If environmental science is ultimately concerned with environmental problem-solving for the sake of achieving a sustainable lifestyle (which I argue is the case), then it seems self-evident that a measure of ethical analysis should be at the core of the environmental sciences. This is a position recognized by Nelson and Vucetich with respect to sustainability science. As they state:

> The critical point is that we cannot understand the role of sustainability science, and hence achieve sustainability, unless we understand the meaning of sustainability, and we cannot understand the meaning of sustainability unless we answer questions like those described above. But we cannot answer such questions without a committed collaboration between sustainability science and environmental philosophy — something that currently does not exist.[19]

In the absence of examining the morality of sustainability, we are unable to parse its meaning. If we cannot parse its meaning then we have no clear conception of the role of sustainability science (or environmental science), and thus have no clear conception of a problem-solving strategy, or frankly of a *raison d'être*.

Unfortunately, environmental science may be drifting toward the positivist camp. This can be illustrated by the evolution of the Advanced Placement (AP) Environmental Science curriculum over the past few years. This is one of several curricula designed to provide college-level course experience for students still in high school. Consider the course outlines for AP Environmental Science for the

---

19 Nelson and Vucetich, 2012.

years 1999 and 2007.[20]

AP Environmental Science Course Outline - 1999

I. Scientific Analysis (5%)
II. Interdependence of Earth's Systems: Fundamental Principles and Concepts (25%)
III. Human Population Dynamics (10%)
IV. Renewable and Nonrenewable Resources: Distribution, Ownership, Use, Degradation (15%)
V. Environmental Quality (20%)
VI. Global Changes and Their Consequences (15%)
VII. Environment and Society: Trade-Offs and Decision Making (5%)
VIII. Choices for the Future (5%)

AP Environmental Science Course Outline - 2007

I. Earth Systems and Resources (10-15%)
II. The Living World (10-15%)
III. Population (10-15%)
IV. Land and Water Use (10-15%)
V. Energy Resources and Consumption (10-15%)
VI. Pollution (25-30%)
VII. Global Change (10-15%)

Close examination of the changes reveals that they go beyond the re-organization of topics. Important additions and subtractions were made. For example, the category "Human Population Dynamics" in 1999 was changed to "Population" in 2007. This reflects the addition of population biology concepts to the curriculum. Such a modification is understandable, and represents a fairly minor alteration taken alone. But other changes surely have had a more substantial impact. In particular I refer to the purging of "Environment and So-

[20] As of this writing, the current AP course outline has remained unchanged since 2007.

ciety" from the topic list. This is the section covering economics, ethics, aesthetics and policy. References to economics and policy can be found sprinkled here and there in the new curriculum, but no systematic effort is made to address the socio-cultural content of environmental problem-solving.

"Choices for the Future" in the earlier iteration of the outline was also eliminated as a category. This section offered teachers and students the opportunity to explore the question of "what kind of world do we want"? Embedded in this question is an invitation to develop a moral compass - not only to define a desired possible future, but to justify it as well. Suggested subjects to be covered include conservation, preservation, remediation, and sustainability. While one can argue about the adequacy of this list, it at least acknowledges the importance of considering long-term goals and their moral foundations as part of what it is to be an environmental scientist. The significance of this transformation of the AP curricula in environmental science cannot be overstated. AP teachers often lack experience in environmental science curricula, and are therefore dependent upon the guidance provided by the College Board outline. They also have an obligation to ensure that students are given every opportunity to acquire the disciplinary knowledge (as determined by the board) to receive college credit. This creates a strong incentive to teach to a test that minimizes, or effectively excludes, socio-cultural factors defining environmental problems. In my opinion, it also gives a skewed and limited understanding of the purpose of environmental science. So, why the shift toward a more positivist educational approach by the College Board?

One possible answer is that environmental science is just too big a field to give justice to all components defining its content. Thus, a strategic decision was made to focus on the more quantifiable elements of environmental problems. That would be an understandable (but not justifiable) solution to a problem defined in terms of having to deal with much more information than can be realistically addressed in a single semester. However, I think a more likely explanation can be deduced from the environmental science course description provided by the College Board. From the section entitled "Laboratory and Field Investigation":

> Because it is designed to be a course in environmental *science* rather than environmental studies, the AP environmental science course must include a strong laboratory and field investigation component.[21]

The AP board is making a clear distinction between environmental science and environmental studies. The implication is that environmental science is not so broadly interdisciplinary as to include the humanities - the proper domain of (non-scientific?) environmental studies programs.

The significance of this re-calibration of environmental science is that it fundamentally alters its essence in a problematic way. For example, if environmental science is about problem solving, why segregate out socio-cultural forces that play such an important causative role in environmental problem generation? How do the changes reflected in the AP environmental science course outline

[21] The College Board, *Environmental Science Course Description*, 2007.

embody an improvement to the curriculum, or a more accurate reflection of purpose? In no way am I attempting to minimize the importance of the physical and natural sciences for the curriculum. I personally would prefer to see greater incorporation of the social together with the natural and physical sciences, but the core of the discipline has always been, and will continue to be, based upon the scientific process. However, no one can plausibly deny that environmental problems are embedded in a socio-cultural milieu. Consequently, scientific understanding can take us only so far. As recognized by the Society for Conservation Biology, environmental and sustainability science also require guidance on the kind of world we are trying to preserve or create, i.e. what does sustainability mean? Without an opportunity to reflect on the question of purpose and/or ends, not only does environmental science risk losing its identity, but society may be less able to measure progress toward addressing a set of challenges that are unprecedented in human history.

To the extent that the new AP environmental science curricula were based upon current undergraduate programs, my fear is that this may reflect a trend in environmental science education generally. If environmental science is truly interdisciplinary, and if environmental problems necessarily require the application of expertise beyond the "hard" or natural sciences, then this curricular pruning is short-changing students in their education, and compromising their ability as problem-solvers to understand and address complex, socially embedded environmental problems. As a result, it may also be compromising our ability as a species to come to terms with a planet in peril.

FINAL THOUGHTS

If asked what I do for a living I always respond in all sincerity that "I am an environmental scientist". Proof comes in the form of having received a doctorate in Environmental Science at a university with "Environmental Science" in its name. As a professor, I have been responsible for teaching several courses in environmental science over the years. I also participated in the development of an environmental science degree-granting program at my university. All this despite not being engaged in traditional research work in the physical or natural sciences that constitute the disciplinary core of environmental science. Instead I have spent most of my academic life considering philosophical questions, especially as they relate to both Aristotle and ecological sustainability.

As outlined in the Introduction, the reason for my chosen path was an inability to adequately answer the question of "Why care?". This was a transformational moment, as I entered my doctoral studies, that pointed me in a completely new and unexpected direction. Thankfully, my advisor was very supportive of my reorientation. My committee never questioned whether a philosophically-focused research agenda was consistent with environmental science as a discipline. This may have been the result of environmental science being relatively new when I was a graduate student. Many of the same people responsible for the creation of environmental science programs in various colleges and universities were still present and likely retained a historical connection to the environmentalist forces that catalyzed the development of the applied disciplines aimed at addressing the many environmental problems being discovered. It was my perception that few, if any, questioned the importance of moral reflection as a means to provide an outline for a sustainable society. This broadly interdisciplinary learning environment both prompted and helped justify my research into Aristotelian philosophy and its potential contribution to helping us better understand the nature of sustainability.

I'm not convinced that the same educational environment exists today, at least not universally. Changes to the AP environmental science course outline suggests that it isn't. As described by Nelson and Vucetich, sustainability science seems to be adrift in the same curricular boat. Such lack of direction comes at exactly the wrong moment, as we face perhaps the most pernicious, unsettling and politically difficult problem in human history - climate change. Our ability to mitigate against a warming world will depend much more on understanding and responding to ideological as opposed to climatological forces. With respect to the United States, the most important factor influencing people's acceptance of human-caused climate change is political affiliation, irrespective of educational attainment.[22] Democrats are much more likely to accept the scientific consensus on climate change and of the need for mitigation efforts than are Republicans. Simply presenting Republican skeptics with climatological evidence, however compelling scientifically, will not be sufficient in the face of an ideologically driven perception that such evidence conflicts with core values, and is thus not to be trusted. An alternative lever must be pulled if progress is sought in

22 Funk and Kennedy, *The Politics of Climate*, 2016.

bringing a larger percentage of the public around to accepting the scientific consensus on climate change, and thus the necessity of taking aggressive action to reduce greenhouse gas emissions.

An example of an alternative approach can be found in the efforts of climatologist Katherine Hayhoe to bridge the gap between science and the religious values constraining most evangelical Christians from accepting the reality of climate change.[23] As an evangelical Christian herself, Hayhoe has sought to demonstrate how the values found within her faith-based community are consistent with efforts to realize environmental sustainability and combat climate change.[24] Reframing ideological/religious values may be a difficult challenge, but is probably our only option in those situations in which the overriding factor affecting our ability to institute positive change is the willingness and capacity to both understand and engage value-driven issues. To the extent that environmental scientists are unwilling or unable to come to terms with this aspect of problem solving significantly reduces their effectiveness.

In my opinion, the task ahead for environmental science is to recapture its more broad-based interdisciplinary roots by re-infusing a healthy dose of the humanities as part of its core. Environmental science need never relinquish the emphasis placed on the physical and natural sciences, but neither should it exclude the humanities as being part of its identity. This does not mean that students should be required to engage in the kind of philosophical analysis represented

23 It should be noted that political values also play an important role in the evangelical worldview, as most Christian evangelicals are Republicans.

24 Hayhoe & Farley, *A Climate for Change*, 2009.

in these pages (although that should be an option). It does entail that students should be exposed to the fundamental questions that brought environmental science into existence in the first place, and propels it into the future. In particular, and with respect to our environmental problem-solving agenda, I think we all would benefit from being tasked with the question of why should we care? If we never address this basic question of purpose, then why bother?

NOTES

Andrew Brennan and Yeuk-Sze Lo, "Environmental Ethics." *Stanford Encyclopedia of Philosophy.* https://plato.stanford.edu/entries/ethics-environmental/.

Rober Brulle, "Politics and the Environment," in *Handbook of Politics: State and Society in Global Perspective*, ed. Kevin T. Leicht and J. Craig Jenkins (New York: Springer-Verlag, 2010).

J. Ronald Engel, "Ethics of Sustainable Development," in *Ethics of Environment and Development*, ed. J. Ronald Engel (Tucson: The University of Arizona Press, 1991).

Cary Funk and Brian Kennedy, "The Politics of Climate." *assets.pewresearch.org.* (October 2016). http://assets.pewresearch.org/wp-content/uploads/sites/14/2016/10/14080900/PS_2016.10.04_Politics-of-Climate_FINAL.pdf.

Katharine Hayhoe and Andrew Farley, *A Climate for Change* (New York: FaithWords, 2009).

J. Donald Hughes, "Ecology of Ancient Greece," *Inquiry* 18(1975): 115-125.

Aldo Leopold, *A Sand County Almanac: With Other Essays on Conservation from Round River* (New York: Random House, 1966).

Carolyn Mechant, *The Death of Nature: Women, Ecology, and the Scientific Revolution* (New York: HarperCollins, 1980).

Bill Moyers, "Welcome to Doomsday," *The New York Review of Books*, (March 24, 2005): 8-10.

John Muir, "Hetch Hetchy Valley," in *The Yosemite* (New York: The Century Company, 1912).

M.P. Nelson and J.A. Vucetich, "Sustainability Science: Ethical Foundations and Emerging Challenges," *Nature Education Knowledge* 3 (10) (2012): 12.

Gifford Pinchot, "Principles of Conservation," in *The Fight for Conservation* (New York: Doubleday, 1910).

Richard B. Primack, *Essentials of Conservation Biology* (New York: Sinauer Associates, 2010).

Mark Sagoff, "Animal Liberation and Environmental Ethics: Bad Marriage, Quick Divorce," *Osgoode Hall Law Journal* 22(1984): 297-307.

Kristin Shrader-Frechette, "Throwing Out the Bathwater of Positivism, Keeping the Baby of Objectivity: Relativism and Advocacy in Conservation Biology," *Conservation Biology* (1996): 912-914.

The College Board, "Environmental Science Course Description." *apcentral.collegeboard.org.* (2013) https://apcentral.collegeboard.org/pdf/ap-environmental-science-course-description.pdf.

UNESCO, *Goals of Development* (Paris: United Nations Educational Scientific and Cultural Organization, 1988).

Lynn White, "The Historical Roots of Our Ecologic Crisis," *Science* 155 (3767)(1967): 1203-1207.

BIBLIOGRAPHY

Ackrill, J. L. "Aristotle on Eudaimonia." In *Essays on Aristotle's Ethics*, edited by A. Rorty, 15-33. Berkeley: University of California Press, 1980.

Annas, Julia. "Self-Love in Aristotle." *The Southern Journal of Philosophy* 27(1989): 1-18.

Attfield, Robin. "Has the History of Philosophy Ruined the Environment?" *Environmental Ethics* 13 (2)(1991): 127-137.

Barnes, Jonathan. *The Cambridge Companion to Aristotle*. New York: Cambridge University Press, 1995.

— .*The Complete Works of Aristotle.* Princeton: Princeton University Press, 1984.

Bhuiyan, A.S.M. Anwarullah. "Is Aristotle's Philosophy Anthropocentric? A Biocentric Defense of the Aristotelian Philosophy of Nature." *Biocosmology-Neo-Aristotelism* 5 (2)(2015).

Brennan, Andrew, and Yeuk-Sze Lo. "Environmental Ethics." *Stanford Encyclopedia of Philosophy,* 2016. https://plato.stanford.edu/entries/ethics-environmental/.

Brown, Lester R. "Launching the Environmental Revolution." In *State of the World 1992*, edited by Linda Starke, 174-190. New York: Worldwatch Institute, 1992.

Brulle, Robert. "Politics and the Environment." In *Handbook of Politics: State and Society in Global Perspective*, edited by Kevin T. Leicht and J. Craig Jenkins. New York: Springer-Verlag, 2010.

Chivian, Eric, and Aaron Bernstein. *Sustaining Life: How Human Health Depends on Biodiversity*. New York: Oxford University Press, 2008.

Costelloe, B.F.C., and J.H. Muirhead. *Aristotle and the Earlier Peripatetics*. New York, NY: Longmans, Green, and Co., 1897.

Ducharme, Alain. "Aristotle and the Dominion of Nature." *Environmental Ethics* 36 (2)(2014): 203-214.

Engel, J. Ronald. "Ethics of Sustainable Development." In *Ethics of Environment and Development*, edited by J. Ronald Engel. Tucson: The University of Arizona Press, 1991.

Funk, Cary, and Brian Kennedy. "The Politics of Climate." *assets.pewresearch.org*. October 2016. http://assets.pewresearch.org/wp-content/uploads/sites/14/2016/10/14080900/PS_2016.10.04_Politics-of-Climate_FINAL.pdf.

Gotthelf, Allan. "Aristotle's Conception of Final Causality." *The Review of Metaphysics* (Philosophy Education Society Inc.) 30 (2)(1976): 226-254.

Hankinson, R. J. "Philosophy of Science." In *The Cambridge Companion to Aristotle*, by Jonathan Barnes, 109-139. New York: Oxford University Press, 1995.

Hargrove, Eugene C. *Foundations of Environmental Ethics.* Englewood Cliffs: Prentice-Hall, 1989.

Harlow, Elizabeth M. "The Human Face of Nature: Environmental Values and the Limits of Nonanthropocentrism." *Environmental Ethics* 14 (1)(1992): 27-42.

Hayhoe, Katharine, and Andrew Farley. *A Climate for Change.* New York: FaithWords, 2009.

Hopper, David H. *Technology, Theology, and the Idea of Progress.* Louisville, KY: John Knox Press, 1991.

Hughes, J. Donald. "Ecology of Ancient Greece." *Inquiry* 18 (1975): 115-125.

Hursthouse, Rosalind, and Glen Pettigrove. "Virtue Ethics." *The Stanford Encyclopedia of Philosophy.* Edward N. (ed.) Zalta. (Winter 2016) https://plato.stanford.edu/entries/ethics-virtue/.

Kraut, Richard. *Aristotle on the Human Good.* Princeton, NJ: Princeton University Press, 1989.

Lear, Jonathan. *Aristotle: The Desire to Understand.* New York: Cambridge University Press, 1988.

Leopold, Aldo. *A Sand County Almanac: With Other Essays on Conservation from Round River.* New York: Random House, 1966.

MacIntyre, Alasdair. *After Virtue.* 3rd. Notre Dame: University of Notre Dame Press, 2007.

Merchant, Carolyn. *The Death of Nature: Women, Ecology, and the Scientific Revolution.* New York: HarperCollins, 1980.

Moyers, Bill. "Welcome to Doomsday." *The New York Review of Books* (March 24, 2005): 8-10.

Muir, John. "Hetch Hetchy Valley." In *The Yosemite.* New York: The Century Company, 1912.

Mulgan, R. G. *Aristotle's Political Theory: An Introduction for Students of Political Theory.* Oxford: Clarendon Press, 1977.

Nelson, M. P., and J. A. Vucetich. "Sustainability Science: Ethical Foundations and Emerging Challenges." *Nature Education Knowledge* 3 (10)(2012): 12.

Nussbaum, Martha. *The Fragility of Goodness: Luck and Ethics in Greek Tragedy and Philosophy.* New York: Cambridge University Press, 1986.

Oele, Marjolein. "Folding Nature Back Upon Itself: Aristotle and the Rebirth of "Physis"." *Philosophy* 58 (2017).

Pinchot, Gifford. "Principles of Conservation." In *The Fight for Conservation*. New York: Doubleday, 1910.

Primack, Richard B. *Essentials of Conservation Biology.* New York: Sinauer Associates, 2010.

Roochnik, David. *Retrieving Aristotle in an Age of Crisis.* Albany: State University of New York Press, 2013.

Sagoff, Mark. "Animal Liberation and Environmental Ethics: Bad Marriage, Quick Divorce." *Osgoode Hall Law Journal* 22: 297-307.

Sandler, Ronald. "Environmental Virtue Ethics." In *The International Encyclopedia of Ethics*, by Hugh LaFollette, 1665-1674. Blackwell Publishing Ltd, 2013.

Sedley, David. "Is Aristotle's Teleology Anthropocentric?" *Phronesis* 36 (2)(1991): 179-196.

Shrader-Frechette, Kristin. "Throwing Out the Bathwater of Positivism, Keeping the Baby of Objectivity: Relativism and Advocacy in Conservation Biology." *Conservation Biology* (1996): 912-914.

The College Board. "Environmental Science Course Description."(2013) *apcentral.collegeboard.org.* https://apcentral.collegeboard.org/pdf/ap-environmental-science-course-description.pdf.

UNESCO. *Goals of Development* (Paris: United Nations Educational Scientific and Cultural Organization, 1988).

Weiner, L. "Of Lice and Men: Aristotles Biological Treatises." *The St. John's Review* 40 (1)(1990): 39-52.

White, Lynn. "The Historical Roots of Our Ecologic Crisis." *Science* 155 (3767)(1967): 1203-1207.

INDEX

COLOPHON

EDITOR Molly Q. Cort

DESIGNER Eric C. Wilder

TYPEFACE Pelago

PAPER Blazer Silk

PRINTING More Vang, Alexandria, VA

This book was made possible, in part, through the generosity of More Vang.